# MADE
# BY
# HAND

# MADE BY HAND

## Searching for Meaning in a Throwaway World

# Mark Frauenfelder

PORTFOLIO

PORTFOLIO

Published by the Penguin Group

Penguin Group (USA) Inc., 375 Hudson Street,
New York, New York 10014, U.S.A.
Penguin Group (Canada), 90 Eglinton Avenue East, Suite 700,
Toronto, Ontario, Canada M4P 2Y3
(a division of Pearson Penguin Canada Inc.)
Penguin Books Ltd, 80 Strand, London WC2R 0RL, England
Penguin Ireland, 25 St Stephen's Green, Dublin 2, Ireland
(a division of Penguin Books Ltd)
Penguin Books Australia Ltd, 250 Camberwell Road, Camberwell,
Victoria 3124, Australia
(a division of Pearson Australia Group Pty Ltd)
Penguin Books India Pvt Ltd, 11 Community Centre, Panchsheel Park,
New Delhi – 110 017, India
Penguin Group (NZ), 67 Apollo Drive, Rosedale, North Shore 0632,
New Zealand (a division of Pearson New Zealand Ltd)
Penguin Books (South Africa) (Pty) Ltd, 24 Sturdee Avenue,
Rosebank, Johannesburg 2196, South Africa

Penguin Books Ltd, Registered Offices:
80 Strand, London WC2R 0RL, England

First published in 2010 by Portfolio,
a member of Penguin Group (USA) Inc.

1   3   5   7   9   10   8   6   4   2

LIBRARY OF CONGRESS CATALOGING-IN-PUBLICATION DATA
Frauenfelder, Mark.
Made by hand : my year of finding meaning in a throwaway world / Mark Frauenfelder.
p.   cm.
Includes index.
ISBN 978-1-59184-332-0
1. Self-reliant living.   2. Sustainable living.   3. Handicraft.   I. Title.
GF78.F73  2010
640—dc22   2010001274

Printed in the United States of America
Set in Baskerville
Designed by Jaime Putorti

**For Carla, Sarina, and Jane**

# CONTENTS

# MADE
# BY
# HAND

# INTRODUCTION:
# ESCAPE TO RAROTONGA

"All the best stories in the world are but one story in reality—the story of an escape. It is the only thing which interests us all and at all times—how to escape."

—A. C. BENSON

On New Year's Day 2003, my wife, Carla, and I were sitting in the garden of a little coffeehouse in Studio City, California, with our notebooks open and pens in hand. We were taking part in a yearly ritual: writing down our goals for the coming year. Usually this was a happy, optimistic exercise. In past years we listed such goals as learning Japanese, improving language skills, learning how to become better cooks, and getting book deals with publishers. But not this year. Thanks to the aftereffects of the dot-com implosion of 2001, we were both in a gloomy mood. One of the magazines I was under contract with, *The Industry Standard,* which covered Internet-based businesses, had itself gone out of business, and other tech magazines I contributed to either had shut down or were circling the drain.

The entire freelance-journalism market was in the dumps, and since Carla and I made our living writing for magazines, we were in the dumps, too. Just a couple of years earlier, in 2000, *The Industry Standard* was publishing monstrous, four-hundred-page weekly issues filled with expensive full-page advertisements. (To this day the magazine holds the record for the most ad pages sold in one year.)

In those giddy days, tech magazine editors were desperate for stories to fill pages, and they were paying top dollar for them. I was able to write about almost any subject that struck my fancy: old stop-motion monster movies, retired science fiction comic book artists, kite-camera enthusiasts. It was wonderful. When I pitched these story ideas to my editors, the only question they'd ask me was "How soon can you give me copy?"

But by 2001, after hundreds of Internet companies with untenable business plans—like Kozmo.com, Den.net, Pets.com, Floo.com, Webvan.com, Boo.com, and Etoys.com—blew through hundreds of millions of dollars, wiping out stunned investors and driving the NASDAQ into freefall, there was hardly anyone left to advertise. Instead of four-hundred-page issues, the *Standard* was reduced to a mere pamphlet, topping out at sixty-four pages. The magazine was running on fumes, and it was becoming painfully clear that easy street was about to become a dead end.

I wasn't too surprised when my *Standard* editor called me one morning that August and warned me to submit my final invoice immediately to avoid having to wait in line with other creditors, who would be lucky to get pennies on the dollar for what they were owed. The magazine, which had burned through $200 million in just a few years, was bankrupt.

"We had a good run," my editor told me, and she was right. The money had paid for my kid's school and our mortgage and had given me confidence that we'd be able to deal with the additional expenses of a second child, which we hoped to have in the near future. But now the flow of cash from that fat pipeline into our bank account slowed to a trickle, and reality began to sink in.

In the days following the news of the *Standard's* demise, I made calls to editors I knew at other magazines. They all told me the same thing: They had a backlog of stories, and even if they were to have an assignment for me, they wouldn't be able to pay the same word rate as in previous months. In my mind's eye, I saw our comfortable lifestyle imploding: no more restaurant takeout several nights a week, no vacations in Hawaii, no new laptop every eight months, no trips to the gourmet supermarket, no weekly gardener to tend to our tropical garden, no endless cavalcade of FedExed products pouring through our front door. We were going to have to do some serious cutting back. As the months wore on, work continued to dwindle, and it became clear that the Internet bubble wasn't going to reinflate anytime soon.

As Carla and I sat in the coffeehouse we began to get serious about a radical idea that we'd been toying with as we'd dealt with our reduced income over the past months: Could it be that the problem was less about how much money we were spending and more about how we were spending our time? As we thought about the things we'd have to give up, we began questioning whether we really wanted to raise our kids in an environment of prepackaged diversions, theme-park rides, trips to the mall, freeway traffic, and incessant e-mails. Was there a better way of life out there, waiting for us to create it?

We wrote down three goals:

1. To take more control of our lives.
2. To cut through the absurd chaos of modern life and find a path that was simple, direct, and clear.
3. To forge a deeper connection and a more rewarding sense of involvement with the world around us.

These goals looked awfully good on paper, but how were we actually going to achieve them? Once the holidays were over, we felt sure that practical necessities and the forces of modern society would thwart our every effort to try a new way to live until we gave up and went back into the same old, overcaffeinated routine of school, work, driving, takeout meals, and weekends filled with kiddie birthday parties at Chuck E. Cheese's.

I'm not sure which of us said it first, but we eventually agreed that the solution was to chuck everything and move to Rarotonga.

- - - - - - - - - -

Rarotonga is a remote island in the South Pacific, part of the Cook Island nation. Measuring six miles end to end, it's about one-fifth the size of the Hawaiian island of Kauai. Carla and I had spent a week in Rarotonga in 1994, and we'd fallen in love with its slow pace, its tropical lushness, and its natural beauty.

Life in Rarotonga, we recalled, was simpler. People expected, and were satisfied by, less. The focus wasn't on getting ahead; it was on communing with nature and sharing music, food, dance, and craft. With its wild splendor, bountiful fruit trees, and lovely weather, the island seemed a place where human beings were meant to live. Plus, there was the exotic appeal: Imagine living on an emerald speck in the middle of the South Pacific, thousands of miles from any continent, where life moves at its own pace—what the locals call "Raro time."

Travel writer Arthur Frommer dubbed Rarotonga the third most beautiful island in the South Pacific, behind Tahiti's Moorea and Bora Bora, and James Michener ranked it above Tahiti in beauty, climate, and the hospitality of the native people. We also remembered with amusement that everywhere you look in Rarotonga, wooden statues of the naked, extremely well endowed god Tangaroa stare back at you; he's even found on their flower-shaped coins. The Rarotongans' dancing, which features fast hip gyrations and erotic gestures, was described as "positively obscene" by a nineteenth-century missionary who had grown accustomed to the more languid Hawaiian hula.

After our first visit to Rarotonga, we occasionally, and only half seriously, had talked about moving there. Living on a tropical island is a common fantasy, of course. Lots of people daydream about cutting ties with their busy, tangled lives and moving to an idyllic island free of traffic jams, screaming car alarms, smog-belching Hummers, random incidents of road rage, billboards, talk radio, graffiti, and other noxious ingredients of urban anxiety. But most people quickly dismiss the fantasy because it's completely impractical. Once you move there, how do you live? Jobs are scarce, and even if you do pick fruit and catch fish to survive, you still need money for a place to live, and to buy clothes and other necessities, no matter how spare your lifestyle.

But on that New Year's Day in 2003, Carla and I realized that we really *could* move to Rarotonga. As freelancers, we could write from anywhere, and living in Rarotonga would cost a lot less than doing so in our Los Angeles suburb. At the very least, a frugal life on a paradisiacal island would be a lot more fun. Instead of picking up our kids from "playdates" and zapping frozen organic soy cheese macaroni in the microwave for dinner, we could be picking mangos and breadfruit, buying taro root and coconuts from people's front porches, and fishing for supper. We'd be experiencing life's moments, rather than trying breathlessly to keep up with our schedules.

The more we talked about it, the more the idea made sense. I was doing various illustrating jobs for newspapers and magazines, and there was no reason I couldn't do them in Rarotonga, as long as the place had Internet connectivity. (It did. It was slow and expensive, but it got the job done.)

We could write articles about living on the island, maybe even get a book deal out of it. We'd stay for a year, and if we liked it, we'd stay longer. The only question left in our minds was "When do we leave?" June seemed to be the right time, after Sarina had finished kindergarten. By then, our new baby (due around the first of April) would be two and a half months old. That gave us about five months to prepare.

We began writing a list of things we needed to do before moving:

1. Sell house
2. Sell car
3. Talk to pediatrician about taking newborn baby to island
4. Get passport for baby
5. Box and store the stuff we don't want to bring with us
6. Find homes for pet lovebird and rabbit
7. Find out how to continue Sarina's education
8. Cancel car insurance, Internet service, electricity, water, gas, newspaper

Next, we started a packing list:

*Baby blankets*
*Baby bottles*
*Breast pump*
*Car seat*
*Computers*
*Computer batteries*
*Computer games*
*DVD player/DVDs*
*Fever thermometers*
*Hair dryer*
*Hats*

*Mosquito nets*
*Mosquito repellent*
*Pacifiers*
*Playpen*
*Portable printer*
*Portable radio*
*Stroller*
*Sun cover for car seat or playpen*
*Sunscreen (regular and infant)*
*Toys*
*Ukulele*
*Video camera*
*Voltage converter plugs*
*Walkie-talkies*

As the months went by, the list grew longer. Much longer. This wasn't a plan for a simpler life. This was a condensed catalogue of the modern conveniences we were trying to escape.

Looking back, I can see that, in addition to mosquito nets and sunscreen, this list contained the seeds of our destruction.

- - - - - - - - -

I began reading up on the Cook Islands. I was especially interested in learning about city folk who had tried doing what we were about to do. I read several books by Robert Dean Frisbie of Cleveland, who in 1920, at the age of twenty-four, headed for the South Pacific. For several years Frisbie wandered from island to island, eventually settling on Pukapuka, one of the Cooks' remote northern islands, in order to live in "a place beyond the reach of the faintest echo from the noisy clamour of the civilised world." There Frisbie ran a trading post and wrote the first of a dozen novels and memoirs of living an unencumbered, rustic life in the South Pacific.

In his later years, Frisbie was befriended by Tom Neale, a sailor from New Zealand who had taken a job at the general store in Rarotonga's capital, Avarua. Like Frisbie, Neale longed to escape the noise and congestion of civilization and live on his own terms. He thought that the only way he could do that was by living alone on an island where no one could tell him what to do. In the early 1950s, egged on by Frisbie (now nearly bedridden from a chronic respiratory ailment), Neale moved to a tiny uninhabited Cook island called Suwarrow and set up house in a little shack that had been built as a World War II monitoring post. He caught fish, raised chickens, and hunted down the feral pigs that tore up his garden at night. His days were filled with hard physical labor, but he was profoundly happy on the island, where he lived, on and off, for sixteen years. He wrote about his time on Suwarrow in his memoir, *An Island to Oneself.*

Neale's and Frisbie's books thrilled me and made me even more excited to move to Rarotonga. But I failed to understand that what they had done and what we were about to do were entirely different things. Neale and Frisbie chose to be responsible for making and maintaining every object and system needed to ensure their survival, while Carla and I were still going to be dependent on others to provide for all our necessities and luxuries. We weren't really changing our behavior; we were just changing our environment.

All I can say is, we didn't understand it at the time. We thought that by living on an island, inhabited by people who lived at a slower place, we'd somehow become that way ourselves.

Over the next five months, we went through our to-do list: selling the house, storing our furniture, selling our car, buying supplies. It was exciting, and we talked about little else. At night, lying in bed, we discussed our plans, hopes, and fears. We talked about how our friends thought we were crazy; we sometimes wondered if they were right. We talked about what needed to be done before we got on the plane and left the United States. The one thing we didn't talk a lot about was what we were going to do once we got there.

We had vague notions that we'd simply spend a lot of time hiking and beachcombing and sitting under palm trees while Sarina explored tidepools and our baby slept in a miniature hammock. Beyond that, we didn't have a plan. Part of the reason for that may have been that we really wanted to escape the crazy schedule of kids' playdates and school functions and other social obligations that raised our stress levels. So the idea of not having a plan appealed to us.

When the day came to leave, our friends Liz and Craig dropped in to help with last-minute details. The amount of gear we had lined up in the hallway surprised them: eight giant roller suitcases, a carry-on for each of us, plus a stroller, a portable crib, and a car seat for the baby. We needed two taxis to take us to the airport—one for the four of us and a van for all the luggage. (That luggage became an anchor that dragged on us for our entire stay in the South Pacific. Carla had packed thirteen pairs of shoes, and she never wore any of them, always either sporting a pair of two-dollar flip-flops she bought in Rarotonga or going barefoot.)

After a twelve-hour flight we landed at Rarotonga's tiny airport, across the road from the ocean, which consisted of a simple airstrip and a one-story building with a blue-and-white wooden sign that read WELCOME TO THE COOK ISLANDS. We were greeted by a group of men wearing floral batik shirts who strummed ukuleles near the immigration inspection line. The blue sky went on forever, patched with just a few white fluffy clouds.

As we found out later, we had just missed a four-day rainstorm.

We found a van large enough to take our luggage and us to the holiday bungalow where we planned to stay until we found a place to rent. It took only about two minutes of looking out the van's window to wipe out any preconceived fantasies we had harbored about island life. We passed a long stretch of diesel tanks, refineries, and warehouses. The main road was clogged with cars and noisy motorscooters. Everywhere we looked, there were signs of neglect and ugliness: rusting oil drums, falling-down cinderblock fences, and small packs of skinny feral dogs trotting along with their tongues hanging out.

We didn't remember any of this from our first visit. It had been there, of course, but we had seen it through tourists' eyes. Now that we were back to stay, in a van that reeked of diesel exhaust, passing little houses on the side of the road with missing windows, rotting roofs, and torn curtains in lieu of doors, five months of romanticized notions flew from our heads and were replaced by one question:

What the fuck had we gotten ourselves into?

Our first impulse was to turn around and get the hell out. Our tickets were open-ended, which meant we could leave anytime we felt like it. But we couldn't do that. The humiliation would be excruciating; we would never be able to face our friends again. More than that, the months of planning and work that we'd put into doing this would have been for nothing. Worst of all, going back home would have meant abandoning a dream that we had come to believe in.

By the time the van dropped us off at the tiny bungalow, the sky was dark gray. As I dragged the luggage in, it started to rain. The baby began to cry. A sleep-deprived, whiny Sarina asked over and over again if we could go to the wind-whipped beach.

— — — — — — — — —

It wasn't that we had an *awful* time in Rarotonga. We just didn't find what we were looking for there. Part of the problem was that we didn't know what we were looking for, other than that we wanted to feel good. Our problems, which we assumed were caused by living in Los Angeles, had taken the plane ride with us. It turned out that *we* were the problem. Moving to a so-called paradise couldn't change things.

In some ways, our life on the island was even poorer than it had been in Los Angeles. We had a hard time making friends because the people who lived there were, understandably, not interested—who wants to invest time in forging a friendship with transients? So we lacked a social network. That too was something we hadn't thought about. Since we'd always had friends and family to give us support when we needed it, we hadn't realized how important a circle of friends could be until we didn't have one.

Sarina missed her friends and complained about it incessantly. Jane, at three months old, needed constant care, and Carla missed being able to hang out with mothers of kids the same age. It was just the four of us, and at times it became stifling, with Sarina insisting on having Carla and me as her constant playmates.

Our daily routine involved one of us playing with Sarina while the other took care of Jane. When Jane napped, one of us would frantically write for an hour while the other played with Sarina. We felt just as time-deprived and stressed out as we'd been in Los Angeles, if not more so.

Still, some of our experiences on the island did hint at a more rewarding way to live. After we'd settled into a small house near the ocean (a house once lived in by Robert Frisbie's daughter, Johnny), we enrolled Sarina in a school and, as a result, became friendly with a family on the island. Lori was a Canadian who had met her husband, John, who was half Rarotongan and half Canadian, while he was doing his stint as a Mormon missionary in Canada. They had eight kids and lived across the street from the school, so we often went over to visit at the end of the school day.

One day I saw Lori impale a coconut on a half-inch steel rod sticking out of the ground before husking the fibrous outer coating. I asked if I could try, and she was happy to let me because she needed a lot of coconut meat for her baking that night. Lori showed me how to get leverage by stabbing the coconut husk onto the rod, then rolling it to peel the husk away.

After husking a half dozen, Lori showed me how to crack the coconuts in half by whacking them with the dull side of a machete (what Rarotongans call a "bush knife"). Her seven-year-old daughter, Neomi, was there to catch the coconut water in a pitcher. Next, Lori demonstrated how to use a coconut-scraping bench, a small wooden surface with a blade protruding from one end. She straddled the bench and scraped the meat of a coconut into a white plastic bowl below the blade. I gave it a try and got the hang of it quickly. Sarina wanted to try it, too, so I let her and was surprised to see how easily she took to it.

That evening, when I went to our landlady's house to pay the rent, I asked her where I could buy a coconut-scraping bench. She told me I would have to go to the junkyard in town and buy a piece of a leaf spring from a broken car, take it to a metal shop to have it forged and get the end serrated, and then take that to a carpenter to have a bench made for it.

"Or," she said, "you can borrow mine." She also gave me a coconut-husking rod, a bush knife, and a bag of wild spinach she had just picked.

For the remainder of our time on the island, coconut harvesting and processing was an almost daily ritual that Carla, Sarina, and I relished. Here's a typical coconut-centric day, as recorded in Carla's journal:

*Mark's goal today is to make coconut cream, which he will then use to make coconut chicken, creamy pasta sauce, and scones from scratch.*

He's recruited Sarina to help him in his mission. They collected fallen coconuts this morning, spotting a few next to our laundry lines, and a couple more scattered around the border of our lawn.

Now Mark and Sarina are out in the front yard, trying to open the fruits, which is no simple matter. The edible part of a coconut is encapsulated by a fibrous shell, which is protected by another, thicker shell that—as Mark has learned—cannot be penetrated by whacking it with a sharp rock.

While Mark pries the outer shells open with his handmade iron-wood spear (which took him two days to carve and sharpen), Sarina sits on the grass with a bush knife in hand, whacking the inner shells in half.

"You could slice off someone's head with one of those knives," I hear Mark say.

"Really?" Sarina squeals.

I flinch as she raises the knife up into the air and wonder if I should interfere. I don't think a bush knife is an age-appropriate tool for a six-year-old. But then she cracks the coconut open, a perfect split, and she and Mark hoot with delight.

Once the coconuts are all opened, the white "meat" needs to be grated. Again, this is no simple matter. It's not something you can do with your ordinary cheese grater. The fruit is tenaciously tough and must be shredded with a coconut scraper. Mark and Sarina argue over who gets to scrape the coconuts, and Sarina wins. She straddles the bench with half a coconut in hand, bends forward, and begins to scrape the inside of the shell against the metal scraper. The moist shreds fall into a bucket. She stops for a moment to peel off her shirt, then continues to grate until she runs out of coconuts.

Mark scoops the white mush into a large piece of cheesecloth and wrings it into a jar, which also contains fresh, clear milk from the coconuts. It's surprising how much liquid squirts out of the cloth.

He's now ready to begin cooking.

*Jane is napping, so I decide to steal Sarina for the afternoon. We head down to the beach and rent a bright orange kayak. The boat has an inch of water that sloshes around our feet as we paddle out to a "motu," or islet. The bottom of the shallow lagoon is patched with huge black spots, which, we soon find out, are clusters of sea cucumbers. Sarina leans way over the boat, almost capsizing us.*

*"What are you doing?" I shout.*

*She laughs and holds up a fat, limp cucumber, as if she'd just won a trophy.*

*We come home famished. Mark walks out to the front yard to greet us, looks up at our palm tree, and by sheer luck witnesses a coconut falling from its top. It thumps to the ground with a force that could crack a skull. His eyes water with amazement, the way Moses may have wept when he witnessed the parting of the Red Sea.*

*I make a mental note to stay clear of that tree when hanging my clothes on the line.*

Looking back, the days we spent being deeply involved with our food—collecting it, extracting it, processing it, and cooking it—were the most memorable and rewarding. It was a luxury to spend all day baking coconut scones or making tortillas and pasta from flour, salt, and eggs. Sure, we still would go out to a restaurant for a quick meal when we were too burned out from a day of hiking in the rain forest or dealing with the kids when they got sick, but coconut days became one of the highlights of our routine. When Sarina's classmates came over, they loved to help us and often offered tips on doing things a better way.

When we left the South Pacific after just four and a half months, beaten by pneumonia, bronchitis, lice, ringworm, toenail fungus, and social isolation, I promised myself I'd come up with a "coconut-day" equivalent in Los Angeles—something that would allow me to slow down, use my hands, and become more engaged with the world around me in a meaningful way. As it turned out, I lucked into something even better.

- - - - - - - - -

As soon as I returned to L.A. I got a call from Dale Dougherty, the cofounder of O'Reilly Media, a technical-books publisher in northern California. Dale was familiar with Boing Boing, the nerd-culture blog I founded in 2000, and we'd chatted a few times on the phone while I was in the South Pacific about an idea he'd had for a general-interest technology-project magazine. Dale had successfully launched a line of books called the "Hacks" series, which offered practical tips and short projects in a variety of areas, such as astronomy, selling things on Amazon, improving one's mental abilities, automating the home, and so on. His idea for a magazine that showed how to make, modify, and repair things appealed to me.

Dale and I met several times to brainstorm. We looked at do-it-yourself magazines from the past—the 1940s through 1960s were a heyday for do-it-yourselfers. *Popular Science* contained quite a few articles devoted to making things such as go-karts from lawn mower engines and modernistic coffee tables from plywood and ceramic tile.

Dale and I noticed that these kinds of projects, along with traditional crafting and homesteading activities, such as gardening, raising chickens, keeping bees, and preserving food, had again become popular, due in large part to the great information-delivery capability of the Web. People were rediscovering the joy of DIY. We decided that the magazine should be a celebration of the kind of making, experimenting, and tinkering that was being chronicled by enthusiasts on the Web. The magazine would showcase the best projects in an attractive format and offer tested, step-by-step instructions for doing them at home. We'd encourage tinkering and experimentation by profiling our favorite "alpha makers"—individuals who have learned how to design and build cool stuff—and by recommending and reviewing tools, guide-books, Web sites, and other resources that people interested in making things could use.

The first issue of *Make* came out in February 2005. Dale and I hoped that the magazine would get ten thousand subscribers in the first year. But we were off by a factor of four: Forty thousand people subscribed. Today the paid circulation is well over a hundred thousand. As editor in chief, I've met hundreds of delightful DIYers over the years. I find their approach to living both refreshing and inspiring. DIYers are not afraid to take responsibility for the creation and maintenance of the things they and their families use, eat, wear, play with, learn from, and live in. In fact, they welcome the challenge of creating, maintaining, and modifying their physical environment.

Eventually, my exposure to DIYers led me to the realization that do-it-yourself activities were an essential, if not central, part of achieving a richer and more meaningful life, a life of engagement with the world. I wanted to learn as much as I could from the alpha makers I'd met through the magazine, so that I could incorporate their lessons into my own life.

One thing I learned is that most alpha DIYers have long, ever-growing, and ever-evolving lists of projects they intend to tackle. So I began to keep a list of the things I wanted to try. I didn't allow fear or lack of experience to prevent me from writing down everything I eventually wanted to accomplish:

*Kill my lawn*
*Plant a vegetable garden*
*Start a fruit-tree orchard*
*Grow mushrooms*

*Raise chickens*

*Throw a house concert*

*Make a cigar-box ukulele*

*Keep bees*

*Make preserved and cultured foods*

*Hack my espresso machine*

*Make a still*

*Make a human-powered electricity generator*

*Tutor my kids in math and science*

*Measure the diameter of the Earth, and the distance from the Earth
 to the moon and from the Earth to the sun*

*Make stilts for my daughters*

*Build a treehouse*

*Make a coffee table*

*Sew and knit clothes for my family*

*Carve wooden spoons*

*Forge aluminum espresso tampers*

*Make a silver ring using precious-metal clay*

*Harvest olives and extract the oil*

This was a long list, and I didn't expect that I would enjoy, or succeed at, everything (and I didn't, as you'll see). I wasn't about to say goodbye to modern life again, as we'd attempted in Rarotonga. Instead, I was looking for a balanced approach that worked for my family and me. By incorporating elements of DIY into our household—for example, raising chickens, keeping bees, growing vegetables, sewing clothes, preserving food, and making simple things out of wood and other materials—I hoped we would become more mindful of our daily activities, more appreciative of what we have, and more engaged with the systems and things that keep us alive and well.

# 1 THE COURAGE TO SCREW THINGS UP

**"I tell myself I will learn more from my mistakes than I ever could by being a submissive follower of instructions and bowing to the dubious authority of some distant and unknown manufacturer."**
**—GEORGE GROTZ, *THE FURNITURE DOCTOR***

When I started working at *Make* and began to meet with the highly skilled individuals who would create DIY projects for the magazine, I never thought I'd learn how to design electronic circuits, build furniture, construct robots, modify bicycles, or make musical instruments myself. I was sure I didn't have that kind of talent. I felt envious of "alpha makers" like William Gurstelle, who once built a taffy-pulling machine for *Make* at my request. (I'd seen one in a movie and thought it would be a fun how-to project.) Envious of Mister Jalopy, who artfully integrated an old-fashioned wooden hi-fi cabinet with a computer to simultaneously play old records and digitize the songs for his iPod. Envious of Charles Platt, who could make anything out of ABS plastic, from a board game to a device for resuscitating victims of cardiac arrest.

Then there was Chris Benton, a professor of architecture at the University of California–Berkeley, who attached remote-control camera rigs to kites for taking aerial photographs. Kim Pedersen, who built a monorail train and elevated track in his backyard in Fremont, California. Billy Hoffman, a teenager who created a magnetic stripe reader to reveal the data stored on his driver's license and credit cards.

What qualities did these people have that I, and millions of others, lacked?

After I spent more time with these DIYers and dozens of others, I learned that they hadn't been born with special talents. Mister Jalopy, who is a kind of artist-hero in the DIY world, knew very little about making things until the day in the 1990s that he made a conscious decision to do whatever it took to become "handy." One of my DIYer friend's hands shake with palsy, yet he manages to use it to assemble intricate mechanisms.

I've met my share of DIYers who've lost fingers from mishaps with power tools. It hasn't stopped them from making stuff.

Their secret isn't so much what they have as what they don't have: a fear of failure. Most people loathe failing so much they avoid trying things that require pushing past their current abilities. It's no coincidence that many of my favorite DIYers either dropped out of or never attended college. A few even dropped out of high school. Maybe they were lucky to have escaped the educational system; in school, mistakes result in punishment in the form of poor grades. Because we've been trained to believe that mistakes must be avoided, many of us don't want to attempt to make or fix things, or we quit soon after we start, because our initial attempts end in failure.

My early forays into DIY certainly did. After a few home-improvement projects in my twenties that resulted in leaky pipes, cracked tiles, and crooked wallpaper, and gardening experiments that led to brown tomato plants surrounded by weeds, I gave up and directed my creative urges to computer-based graphic design and illustration, where the UNDO key makes it easy to back out of mistakes.

Making things confounded me, which in part explains my considerable respect for people who do know how to fix things around the house, knit clothes, work on cars, or build things from scratch like go-karts and remote-controlled model airplanes. Though I wasn't a DIYer, my admiration for the breed paid off careerwise. As editor in chief of *Make,* I developed a knack for knowing which projects our readers would enjoy. I was satisfied with helping contributors write their articles and present their projects in an attractive, accessible way.

After I got to know Mister Jalopy, he knocked me out of this comfortable rut.

— — — — — — — — —

I became acquainted with Mister Jalopy (he doesn't use his real name in public) through the tool reviews he submitted for the first issue of *Make.* I was charmed by his perspective of the world as a hackable platform, something to be remade and remodeled to his exacting, eccentric, yet infectiously appealing aesthetic sensibilities. His first *Make* review was for a screwdriver kit that came with fifty-seven different tamperproof screw bits that would, as he put it, "open damn near every machine meant to remain unopened."

Intrigued, I visited Mister Jalopy's blog (hooptyrides.com) and saw a couple of photos of his workshop, brimming with his garage-sale treasures. (Jalopy goes garage-saling every Saturday in the "deep sea suburbia" of Los Angeles's San Fernando Valley.) I e-mailed him and asked if we might photograph his shop for the magazine. He agreed and gave me his address.

My wife, Carla, a part-time photographer, accompanied me to Mister Jalopy's tidy house on a tree-lined street in Burbank. He was in front of his garage, stripping the varnish off a wooden desk he'd picked up, naturally, at a garage sale. A tall man in his midthirties, he had longish black hair and wore wire-rimmed glasses and Levis paired with a Western-style shirt.

I eventually figured out that this was his unwavering personal dress code.

A rusted Mercedes Benz, circa 1960, sat in the driveway. On top of it rested a large gasoline sign rescued from a closed filling station. Parked next to the Mercedes was a wood-paneled station wagon, which Mister Jalopy was tricking out for amateur drag racing. On closer inspection I noticed that the "wood paneling" was actually a custom paint job, not the vinyl wood-grain decal typically applied at the factory. Mister Jalopy told me that he'd hired his neighbor, a retired sign painter for Disney, to paint it for him. When I looked closely, I saw that the knotholes and grain patterns of the painted wood were filled with images of monster eyeballs, spiders, and other creatures.

Mister Jalopy led Carla and me into the garage. Eye-catching bric-a-brac covered every square inch. On the floor were a miniature gray race car salvaged from a 1930s kiddie ride, four bright yellow magnesium racing wheels from Barney Navarro's 1967 Indy 500 car, a vintage O'Keefe & Merritt stove (painted turquoise with racing pinstripes), the aforementioned art deco Farnsworth radio cabinet fitted with a Macintosh-based album digitizing system, and a Captain Fantastic pinball machine Mister Jalopy had found abandoned on the side of the road. After tussling over it with a drunk homeless man, he had victoriously brought it home for restoration.

The garage was a personal expression of Mister Jalopy's philosophy. In his world, the things around you should have meaning, and his way of giving them meaning is by collecting, customizing, rebuilding, and combining them in ways that make him happy. Standing there in his garage, looking at his chests of hand tools, Model T headlights, art nouveau lamp stands, cast-iron cookware, old countertop-advertising mascot statuettes, and other cleaned-up, refinished, and remixed garage sale finds, I suddenly very much wanted to do what he was doing. I don't mean that I wanted to copy his aesthetic sensibility (though much of it resonated with me); I just wanted to gain that kind of control over my environment and the things in it. To make my space mine.

We hit it off that day and became friends. I eventually asked him to explain his knack for turning other people's trash into treasure. "People think it's unusual, what I do," he said after a lengthy pause. "I don't even think of it as what I do. I'm just living. What I do is the same as cooking or gardening. The difference is the perception of the barrier to entry. People are afraid that they're going to screw something up, that they're going to ruin something. And unfortunately, it's valid—they will. You *will* screw stuff up. Things *will* be broken. But that's the one step to overcome to get on the path of living this richer life of engagement, of having meaningful connections to the objects around you. It's that necessary step you have to take—the courage to screw things up—so you're able to fix things, or to make stuff from scratch, or to refurbish stuff to live according to your standards."

Mister Jalopy's answer made me feel both ashamed and inspired. Ashamed because he was dead-on about my own fear of screwing things up and the cop-out rationalizations that ran through my head whenever I considered doing something myself: "I'll mess it up." "Experts can do it better, faster, and cheaper than I can." "I might electrocute myself, poison myself, lose or break a body part, or get blown up." Whether he knew it or not, Mister Jalopy was prodding that helpless and insecure part of me that balked at the challenge of DIY. But his answer also inspired me, because I now felt like I had permission to make mistakes, to break things, to fail.

What I've learned from Mister Jalopy and other DIYers is

that mistakes are not only inevitable—they're a necessary part of learning and skill building. Mistakes are a sign that you're active and curious. In fact, recent brain research suggests that making mistakes is one of the best ways to learn.

While there's nothing wrong with striving to become an excellent craftsman who can do no wrong (if such a person exists), most of the broad-spectrum DIYers I know tend to *honor* their mistakes, not hide them. Tom Jennings—the skate-punk hacker who founded *Homocore* (a queer zine in the 1980s), invented Fidonet (the way pre-Web bulletin-board systems sent data to one another), cofounded the world's first Internet service provider (The Little Garden), and rebuilt a Data General Nova 4/X minicomputer system in his living room, among many other insanely inventive creations combining software and scavenged electronics—wrote an article for an early issue of *Make* about failure as the great teacher.

"No one talks of failure as anything but shameful; this is wrongheaded and foolish," he wrote. "Mistakes are synonymous with learning. Failing is unavoidable. Making is a process, not an end. It is true that deep experience helps avoid problems, but mainly it gives you mental tools with which to solve inevitable problems when they come up." He argued that "the act of failing again and again" is the only way to equip oneself with the mental toolbox of a successful DIYer.

Jennings and Mister Jalopy, among other DIYers, appreciate the useful and beautiful aspects of their home-built objects, but they also hold the irregularities and flaws of their creations to be admirable qualities, the qualities that make them stand out from smooth and shiny mass-produced commodities. It touches on the Japanese concept of *wabi sabi*, the beauty found in an object's imperfections.

# HOW CIGARETTE ADVERTISING KILLED DO-IT-YOURSELF

Before the 1920s, people in the United States and Europe were more like Mister Jalopy and Jennings. But instead of being DIYers by choice, they did it themselves out of necessity. In those days, when people bought something—a butter churn, an electric fan, a power tool—they expected to maintain it. Fortunately, things in those days were built to be fixable by the owner. They didn't yet come with those condescending NO USER SERVICEABLE PARTS INSIDE stickers affixed to them. They were easy to open, easy to tinker with. They had instructions printed on them. They either came with the tools needed to keep them in working order or were compatible with standard tools.

If you owned a Model T (produced from 1908 to 1927), you were expected to be a mechanic as well as a driver, making repairs as necessary—especially to the tires, which blew out often. This wasn't an unreasonable assumption on the part of the Ford Motor Company, because a large percentage of the people who bought Model Ts had experience maintaining farm machinery. The only tools you needed to repair a Model T were a wrench, a hammer, a screwdriver, and pliers. According to a Smithsonian Institution exhibition called "America on the Move," Model T owners boasted that they could fix their cars with "twine, baling wire, or clothespins." For these people, do-it-yourself was a way of life.

Until Sigmund Freud's nephew killed it.

Edward Bernays is widely regarded as the creator of modern emotion-based advertising. Bernays used his famous uncle's ideas about the drives and desires surging below the surface of our rational, fact-based consciousness to brainwash millions of people into becoming consumers instead of makers and fixers. Born in Vienna in 1891, Bernays moved to the United States as a young man and became Enrico Caruso's press agent. Soon he was selling his public relations services to major corporations around the world. In a few years he managed to change the way people felt about being self-reliant.

He did this by persuading people to buy products and proposals through tantalizing depictions of fantasy worlds that stoked their unconscious urges, instincts, and sexual impulses. His campaigns sidestepped rational thought, appealing to the subconscious parts of the mind—the parts immune to logical argument. The best part about Bernays's technique (to the manufacturers who hired him) was that no matter how much stuff people bought, they never felt satisfied. Like a mirage, the promise of fulfillment seemed alluringly attainable but remained always just out of reach.

In 1917 the U.S. government hired Bernays to sell a dubious public on the idea that the nation needed to enter the Great War. Bernays coined the slogan "Make the world safe for democracy." It worked. When the war ended, Bernays was invited to attend the Paris Peace Conference with Woodrow Wilson, where the president was welcomed as a liberator. Bernays wrote in his 1928 book, *Propaganda*, "The astounding success of propaganda during the war . . . opened the eyes of the intelligent few in all departments of life to the possibilities of regimenting the public mind. . . . If we understand the mechanism and motives of the group mind, is it not possible to control and regiment the masses according to our will without them knowing it?"

In the 1930s, Philco hired Bernays to increase the sales of radios. At the time radios were considered something that only people in lower socioeconomic classes owned. To counteract this perception, Bernays orchestrated a black-tie gala at the gallery in Rockefeller Plaza to promote the radio as a status symbol. He also convinced high-end architects to design houses with radio-listening rooms. As a result, "radio, a toy of the unwashed, became the musical instrument of the affluent," said Bernays.

Bernays's proudest accomplishment was the creation of a nation of female tobacco addicts in the 1920s. George Washington Hill, then president of the American Tobacco Corporation, hired Bernays to persuade women to take up smoking. At the time, women bought just 12 percent of the cigarettes in America. "If I can crack that market," Hill told Bernays, "I'll get more than my share of it. It will be like opening a new gold mine right in our front yard." Hill wanted to promote the idea with a slogan Hill had developed: "Reach for a Lucky instead of a sweet."

Bernays, who was well-connected in the media, asked photographer friends to take photos of slim, pretty women smoking. He also paid physicians to go on record stating that cigarettes were an important part of a meal because the smoke "disinfects the mouth and soothes the nerves." But Bernays, genius that he was, didn't stop there. He knew that in order to succeed on a grand scale, he must change the environment in which women spent their every waking hour. He persuaded restaurants to offer cigarettes on their dessert menus as a substitute for calorie-rich sweets. He got furniture makers to fit kitchen cabinetry with compartments for storing cigarettes and houseware manufacturers to make cigarette tins (with matching flour and sugar tins). He wanted cigarettes, and the opportunities to smoke them, to be ubiquitous.

Through Bernays's efforts, women had started to smoke at home and in restaurants, but shouldn't they, like men, be smoking in the streets, too? (At the time, smoking in public was considered unladylike, and women were reluctant to join men in lighting up on the corner.) Coming up with the strategy of equating smoking with freedom, Bernays orchestrated a stunt in which a large group of attractive young women smoked in public at the Easter

Day Parade in New York. Bernays tipped off the press that a group of suffragettes was planning to publicly make a stand for independence by igniting "torches of freedom." What he didn't tell the press is that he had hired the psychoanalyst A. A. Brill to help him understand the psychology of smoking and how it could be applied to the art of subliminal influence. Brill told Bernays that cigarettes were symbolic penises. (Bernays's uncle would have told him the same for free, I'll bet.) By combining the idea of empowerment and freedom with symbolic penises, Bernays's plan was a hit. The press was on hand to photograph the staged event, and as soon as the images appeared in the newspapers, cigarette sales skyrocketed. By the end of 1928, American Tobacco's annual revenue increased by $32 million (about $400 million in today's money, adjusted for inflation) over the previous year.

This outdoor-smoking stunt was emblematic of the new trend in advertising, which appealed to people's subconscious, irrational desires instead of their actual needs. Today advertising that links emotions to products is so prevalent that no one is surprised when advertisers tie subconscious urges with every kind of nonessential mass-produced product imaginable, from coffeemakers to motorcycles. Even though the techniques used to light up our ids were revealed long ago, they are just as effective now as they were when Bernays introduced them more than eighty years ago. That's because our ids can't listen to reason but can only (as Freud described it) "[strive] to bring about the satisfaction of the instinctual needs."

The problem, of course, is that smoking cigarettes won't ever make you free. But as long as advertisers continue to target the subconscious with the idea that products and freedom are one and the same, people will buy more and more in a desperate effort to achieve independence.

Bernays went on to work with corporations to sell cars to men and magazines to women on the promise that consuming them would boost their sex appeal.

In *The Century of the Self,* Adam Curtis's 2002 BBC Four documentary about the history of using psychological-control techniques to engineer public consent, Peter Strauss, who worked for Bernays from 1948 to 1952, said,

*Eddie Bernays saw the way to sell product was not to sell it to your intellect—that you ought to buy an automobile—but that you will feel better about it if you have this automobile. I think he originated that idea that they weren't just purchasing something—that they were engaging themselves emotionally or personally in a product or service. It's not that you think you need a piece of clothing but that you will feel better if you have a piece of clothing. That was his contribution in a very real sense. We see it all over the place today but I think he originated the idea, the emotional connect to a product or service.*

The financial industry, which was capitalizing factories and department store chains in the 1920s, recognized the value of what Bernays had to offer. Paul Mazur of Lehman Brothers emphasized the need to "shift America from a 'needs' to a 'desires' culture. People must be trained to desire; to want new things even before the old could be entirely consumed."

## SEEING THROUGH THE ILLUSION

And so it goes today. People buy things because the multibillion-dollar advertising industry hires some of the smartest and most creative people on the planet to create irresistible ads that are effective even when people know they are being hoodwinked. Bernays laid the groundwork for today's advertisers. They have it easier than he did. In Bernays's time, advertisers had to convince people that homemade clothing was shameful, home-canned food unsanitary, and old cars symbols of failure. Today's consumers are already conditioned to throw away perfectly good TVs, computers, and MP3 players to make room for the latest model.

It's not easy to see through the consensual illusion that buying stuff will make you happy. But the people I've met through *Make* have succeeded, to one degree or another, in deprogramming themselves of the lifelong consumer brainwashing they've received. They've learned how to stop depending so much on faceless corporations to provide them with what they need (and desire) and to begin doing some of the things humans have been doing for themselves since the dawn of time. They're willing to take back some of the control we've handed over to institutions. They believe that the sense of control and accomplishment you get from doing something yourself, using your own hands and mind, can't be achieved in any other way. They make things not because they are born with a special talent for making but because they choose to develop and hone their ability. And yes, some of the things they make are mistakes, but they aren't afraid of making them, because they've rejected the lesson from the Bernays school of brainwashing that says handmade stuff is bad because it isn't perfect.

The alpha DIYers I have gotten to know over the years have inspired me to make things and make mistakes. Once I discovered how much fun it was to become active in the process of making, maintaining, and modifying the things I use and consume every day, the little flaws, quirks, and imperfections in my handiwork stopped becoming shameful and instead felt like badges of honor.

# 2 KILLING MY LAWN

> "The greatest fine art of the future will be the
> making of a comfortable living from a small piece
> of land."
> —ABRAHAM LINCOLN

In 1978 a Tasmanian field biologist named Bill Mollison and his student David Holmgren published a self-sufficiency guidebook called *Permaculture One: A Perennial Agriculture for Human Settlements.* The book offers instructions for designing small-scale agricultural systems that are able to use waste products (instead of purchased fertilizers, herbicides, and livestock feed) as raw materials. *Permaculture* meant "permanent agriculture," but Mollison later said it could also mean "permanent culture," because this type of agriculture has a lasting ripple effect on many other aspects of the lives of its practitioners.

Mollison was born in 1928 and spent much of his early career studying the different ecosystems of Australia and Tasmania, paying special attention to the mutually beneficial relationships among the things that lived in them. In 1959 he designed a system that defined plants, trees, and marsupials as "components" that interacted with one another in Tasmanian rain forests.

As a result of this work, Mollison had a revelation: Nature's components could be snapped together like Tinkertoy pieces to create thriving ecosystems that provided fuel for heat, food for people and livestock, and materials that could be used for construction, clothing, furniture, and other needs.

To give an example of how components can be connected in a simple way, consider the "three sisters" companion-planting method for growing beans, squash, and maize. Cornstalks provide natural climbing poles for beans, beans add nitrogen to the soil (an essential ingredient that many plants deplete), and squash's broad, prickly leaves provide ground cover to prevent the soil from drying out and discourage vermin from raiding the crop. The three-sisters method saves effort (not having to make a beanpole or spread mulch) and money (for insecticide, fertilizer, and water).

Over the years, Mollison, Holmgren, and a growing legion of "permies" have continued to develop the process of designing small-scale ecosystems that are beneficial to humans. I became interested in permaculture when my friend Terry Miller, who ran *Make*'s Web site at the time, told me about a weeklong class on the subject she'd taken in northern California. After hearing about the things she'd done there, I fantasized about turning my house and property into an experimental permaculture lab, with bees, chickens, and a garden, all connected in a way that let nature do the heavy lifting while I harvested the bounty.

In a permie paradise, "nuisances" like bugs, deadwood, and rotten fruit become valuable resources. Grass clippings become nutrient-rich fodder for the compost pile; fallen leaves can be raked up and turned into mulch, to be spread on top of gardens to conserve water and inhibit weed growth. Terry Miller lays burlap feed sacks under the elevated wire-mesh floor of her chicken coop. After a couple of weeks, she removes a well-fertilized sack and lays it over the soil of one of the potted fruit trees on her deck. That way, when she waters the tree, the chicken droppings dissolve into the soil, providing nitrogen and other minerals.

David Holmgren, cofounder with Mollison of the permaculture movement, developed a seven-step design process for establishing a permaculture system, encapsulated in the mnemonic O'BREDIM: observation, boundaries, resources, evaluation, design, implementation, and maintenance. The first five steps, which require little or no physical labor, are the most important ones and require at least a year to complete, if done correctly. They require careful observation of your land, watching what happens to it over four seasons. At the observation stage, you're supposed to study what kinds of plants grow in different locations, where water tends to collect, what the soil conditions are, and how different parts are affected by the sun, wind, shadows, wildlife, and rain.

After becoming intimate with the land and the way it changes over the course of the seasons, you make a map of it, establishing its boundaries and topography. Next, you take stock of your resources: How much time, money, equipment, and materials do you have? The information gathered from the first three steps—observation, boundaries, resources—is then evaluated before going on to the single most crucial step: design. This is where you create a plan to harness sunlight to create complexity out of chaos, providing you and your family with the things you need to survive. Only after these five steps are complete should you even start making your permaculture system.

In theory, Holmgren's plan makes sense. But I had no intention of following it to the letter—I wanted a garden, chickens, and bees as soon as possible. I figured that having lived in the same house (a 1930 farmhouse in the Melody Acres section of Tarzana) for more than three years counted for something as far as steps one through three were concerned. I spent a good couple of hours on step four—evaluating—before moving on to step five—design—which amounted to eyeballing where the raised-bed planters and the beehive would go. I was almost ready to move to the fun part—implementation. But first I had to kill my lawn.

In August 2008, after having read a few books like *Edible Estates* and *Food Not Lawns*—which were about converting front lawns into vegetable gardens—I decided to get rid of my own front lawn. My entire yard was about a half acre, and my front yard constituted roughly a quarter of that. That was sufficient to provide the blank slate on which to build my own permaculture system. As I learned from these books, lawns were invented centuries ago by moneyed Europeans as a way to show off the fact that they didn't *need* to use their land for farming—similar to the way a peacock's tail feathers advertise to potential mates that he can survive despite such a cumbersome fashion statement. Eventually, lawns caught on among the less well-off, including homeowners in the United States, who today spend billions watering, mowing, fertilizing, and resodding ground they don't actually use.

In early August I took a one-day course called "Killing Your Lawn." Steve Gerischer, a landscape designer with a trim mustache, taught the course. Standing on the elevated stage of a community center in front of a couple of hundred people in Altadena, California, he began by saying that if you approach gardening as problem solving, "it will rapidly become a bore." Instead, he advised, look at it as an opportunity to try stuff out. "Ask yourself, 'What do I get to do?' not 'What do I have to do?'" Good advice for any DIY pursuit, actually.

Gerischer said he killed his own lawn years ago, not for any of the "right" environmental reasons but because he loves growing plants and needed enough square footage to grow "one of everything." In the process, he learned that removing your lawn and replacing it with a garden was good for the planet. "One hour of running a poorly tuned lawnmower equals 340 miles driven in a new car," he said. "Fifty-four million households get out each weekend to mow, blow, and edge, using 800 million gallons of gas per year, mostly in the spring and summer, when we are the most air-quality challenged." The audience moaned as Gerischer rattled off these and other facts about the evils of lawns.

Next, he listed the different ways to kill a lawn. You can rip out the grass with tools, which is hard work but effective if you do it right. You can kill it with chemicals like Roundup, but you run the risk of killing your existing vegetable garden if the herbicide drifts over to it in the breeze. The third option is smothering it by covering it with plastic, or with newspaper and cardboard.

Death by newspaper appealed to me because it seemed cheaper, easier, and less toxic than the other methods. I'd been saving newspapers since hearing about the method a couple of months earlier. Gerischer said that after laying down the newspapers, you could then cover them with mulch. When it came time to plant, you just poked holes through the newspaper.

The next day I called a topsoil and mulch supplier in Orange County. Sandy, the woman who answered the phone, was polite and helpful. She told me that mulch prices started at $19 per cubic yard and ran all the way up to $59. The expensive stuff, she said, was a chocolate brown "path mulch" made primarily from tree bark.

I debated which kind of mulch to buy. It was tempting to buy the cheap stuff, but then I remembered what had happened a week earlier, when I bought a durable black plastic garden cart in anticipation of hauling mulch around. When Carla saw it, she literally groaned at how ugly it was. "Why couldn't you have bought a metal wheelbarrow with wood handles?" she asked. I explained that I had found the plastic cart on Amazon, liked the reviews, and clicked BUY.

The plastic cart exemplified Carla's major complaint about my DIY projects. She was concerned that my amateurish activities would result in more eyesores. As editor in chief of *Craft* magazine (the sister publication to *Make*) she had high standards for aesthetic appeal. "If it looks bad," she warned me more than once, "I'm going to hire someone to rip it out and do it the right way."

With the sting of the garden cart still in my mind, I told Sandy to send me the $59-a-yard mulch. She recommended I get enough to cover my lawn two inches deep. That meant I'd need about thirteen cubic yards. I ordered fifteen just to be safe. I also ordered a fifty-pound bag of gypsum, which Gerischer told me to scatter on the grass before I laid down the cardboard and newspaper, as it would accelerate the process. The total price, including delivery, was $971. It seemed like a lot, but I figured it would pay for itself in a couple of years through reduced water bills.

Two days later a ZZ Top look-alike drove up in a dump truck. I asked him to drop the load on the driveway. Unfortunately, the telephone wires above it were too low and would get snagged on his truck if he drove past our front gate into the yard. "Dump it in front of the house," I told him. This meant I'd have to wheel cartfuls of mulch through the gate and down the driveway to the front yard, but I didn't have any other choice. The driver positioned the truck and tilted the bed. As the mulch poured out, a cloud of choking, dark dust rose up and turned my clothes a deep shade of ochre. The mulch was filthy! Before the dust had even settled, the truck had vanished down the road, leaving me standing next to a $1,000 pile of dirty tree bark.

Carla was concerned that someone would steal the mulch. "It costs a lot of money," she said. "People are going to take it. The guy should have put it behind our fence. You better spread it on the lawn right away."

The next morning, as I drove my kids to day camp, I noticed a sizable dent in the mulch pile. Someone had helped themselves to it overnight.

That afternoon I was ready to get started, but then I remembered Gerischer had advised pouring full-strength vinegar on the lawn before laying down the newspaper as another good way, along with the gypsum, to jumpstart the lawn-killing process. I drove to Costco and bought four one-gallon jugs of vinegar. I also grabbed as much cardboard from the free bin at Costco as I could fit into my VW Beetle.

When I returned home, I broke open the bag of gypsum and sprinkled it on the lawn. It turns out that fifty pounds of powder makes for a very light dusting when spread over as much lawn as we had. The vinegar went even faster. I had to dilute it with a lot of water to stretch it out. The entire lawn ended up with a light drizzling of a liquid that was about 25 percent vinegar. (When I went back and reviewed my notes from the class I took, I read that Gerischer had said to drench the grass with about an inch and a half of vinegar, measured in the way that rainfall is determined. That would have been about thirteen gallons.)

Already I'd learned two things about lawn killing: Don't order mulch unless you inspect it for cleanliness first (I've heard reports of mulch contaminated with broken glass and dog shit), and buy plenty of vinegar. This is the problem with DIY projects. You end up learning a lot when you do something the first time, but unless you want to tear it down and start over, you have to live with the mistakes you make. I guess I could have bought more vinegar, but I thought I should get started before the mulch thief returned for another load.

I began covering the lawn with layers of newspaper. The slightest breeze would send the sheets flying from where I'd placed them, so I carried a watering can with me to wet down the paper as I worked. After I'd laid down a couple of rows, I'd fill the wheelbarrow with mulch and spread it over the papers.

During one of my wheelbarrow trips to the mulch pile, a middle-aged woman in a purple sweat suit, thick red hair spilling out from under a cap, introduced herself as the house sitter from next door. Smiling artificially, she told me the owners were selling the house and had moved out; she was watching it for them.

"Look at all that mulch," she remarked.

"Yes, I'm using it to cover my front lawn," I said.

"I need some of it for a garden I'm growing," she said. "I'll come get it later."

"Well," I muttered, "if it's just a little."

"I'm not sure if there's a wheelbarrow at the house, though," she said. "Can I come over later and borrow yours?"

"I guess so."

She walked away.

I told Carla about the strange encounter, and she told me to stop what I was doing and spend the rest of the evening moving the pile of mulch behind the gate, where no one could get their hands on it. It took me a couple of hours to transfer the entire pile, one wheelbarrow at a time. I had to wear a painter's mask so I wouldn't inhale the dust, which covered my clothes in a dark red-brown layer. (Fortunately, our next-door neighbor never came back. Maybe my unenthusiastic response turned her off.)

The next day, Carla helped me lay down newspapers and spread mulch. I think she felt sorry for me, having watched me move a mountain of mulch from one place to another. I was happy that she was pitching in. But her mood was skeptical. "I really don't think this is going to work," she said.

"Why not?" I asked her.

"You don't know what you're doing, that's why."

"But I took that class!" I said.

"We'll see."

But as she worked her attitude improved. The fact that she was helping—and therefore had some skin in the game—made her more hopeful that it would work.

By the end of the second day, we had succeeded in covering about a third of the lawn with mulch. I was bored. I enjoyed the physical exertion of pitchforking the mulch into the garden cart and dumping it, but the tedium of laying down the newspaper was getting to me. I didn't like crawling on my hands and knees and constantly pouring water onto the sheets of paper to keep them from blowing away. It took about twenty minutes to do a row. When I estimated that I had about thirty more rows to go, I sighed.

After a week or so I was about 75 percent done. At this point I had fallen into a routine that wasn't entirely unpleasant. I'd learned to work in the morning, when it was cooler (110-degree afternoons were the norm for Tarzana in August) and there was less of a breeze (so the papers would stay put). I'd found a way to lay down the newspapers more efficiently and without having to get on my knees, and I was using a hose with a mist nozzle to wet the papers instead of a watering can that needed frequent refilling. When I dumped a cartload of mulch onto the papers, I was able to expertly kick the pile around to get an even layer onto the lawn. I wouldn't want to spend the rest of my life as a professional mulch spreader, but I now had the skills to make it easier if I wanted to mulch another section of my lawn or to help a friend do it.

## WAR WITH THE RHIZOMES

Several weeks after I had laid the mulch down, the Bermuda grass underneath it started sprouting through. Carla noticed the patches one morning as she was loading the kids into the car for school.

"That looks awful," she said. "We should have used Roundup."

"I've been pulling up the grass a little every day," I replied.

This was more or less true. Most days, I'd spend a few minutes yanking up the grass whenever I happened to walk by to collect the mail or water the garden. Once in a while, I'd get more ambitious and crawl across the lawn, pulling out clumps at a time.

"It looks like you're fighting a losing battle," she said.

The Bermuda grass *was* a challenging opponent. If it had a credo, it might be Matthew's line from the Bible "He that endures to the end shall be saved."

Also known as devil grass, wire grass, and dogtooth grass, Bermuda grass was brought to the United States in the mid-eighteenth century from Africa (although it probably originated in India, where is was fed to sacred cows) and spread quickly through the South and to the rest of the country. This fast-growing, tenacious plant has outwitted hungry animals and punishing climate swings, sinking its fibrous, six-foot-long roots into the ground and evolving segmented blades that break off like a lizard's tail at the slightest tug, growing back with a vengeance. Bermuda grass flourishes in both acidic and alkaline soil and can even tolerate salty water. During periods of severe drought, it goes into a semidormant state, patiently biding its time until the rain returns. It's the first plant to grow back when an African savannah burns.

Steve Gerischer had warned me that Bermuda grass was the lawn killer's biggest obstacle. Unless you adopt a scorched-earth policy, dousing your lawn with herbicide, Bermuda grass will spring back. The only solution for those who insist on going the organic route is to pull up the grass as soon as it pokes out of the mulch. "If you keep at it, you will eventually exhaust the roots," Steve said.

I took the eradication of the Bermuda grass as a challenge. If I couldn't beat a weed, how would Carla ever consent to my planting an orchard or keeping bees? I just couldn't allow grass to outwit me.

Bermuda grass does possess a certain kind of vegetable intelligence that has allowed it to survive in the harshest of conditions. Its long shoots, called rhizomes, creep along horizontally between the ground and the layer of newspapers and mulch, feeling their way for weak spots. When they find one, they make a right-angle turn, shoot up, and start converting sunlight into chemical energy, which they send to the roots. The replenished roots use this energy to send out new rhizomes to find more weak spots in the mulch barrier. I knew that I had to stay on top of this problem or else it would quickly grow out of control.

As the weeks went by the Bermuda grass and I entered a battle of wills. Once, when I slacked off for three days, a bumper crop broke through the mulch, prompting Carla to ask, "Can you work on that grass after dinner? It's getting really big and bushy out there." I fantasized about buying a hundred gallons of vinegar and drenching the mulch with it. That would teach the grass not to mess with me. But I resorted to hours of hands-and-knees work, and by fall the Bermuda grass cried uncle. I had conquered the weed.

# 3 GROWING FOOD

In September, as my battle with the Bermuda grass was winding down, I turned my attention to my vegetables. A few weeks earlier, I'd germinated about forty different kinds of vegetable seeds in a starter kit on the counter of our kitchen's bay window. Unfortunately, the light from the window was weak, and as a result, the stems grew long and spindly and were pinched in spots like a kinked garden hose. They'd exhausted themselves in a mad search for sunshine. Eventually, all but five plants died. I was left with three Japanese cantaloupes and two Moon and Stars watermelons. Even these survivors had skinny, floppy stems. I didn't have high hopes for their survival.

I had four types of tomatoes already growing in the small garden next to the driveway, as well as peppers, cucumbers, and a variety of squash. The Roma tomatoes were ripe and ready to harvest. I picked one from the vine and bit off a big chunk. It was mealy, spongy, thick skinned, and devoid of flavor. I spat it out and threw it onto the compost pile. I tried another, and another. They all tasted like lousy grocery-store tomatoes. I blamed this on Home Depot, where I'd bought the seedlings.

I'd never given much thought to vegetable seeds before, but once I started to take gardening seriously, I realized how important seed selection is. Seed DNA plays a big role in the taste, hardiness, and appearance of the plants. Hybrid seeds, which come from artificially cross-pollinated plants, have been bred for high yields, disease resistance, and long shelf life. The seeds hybrid plants produce aren't identical to the ones they grew from, and the vegetables they produce are usually inferior in taste or size. In other words, you have to buy new hybrid seeds every year.

On the other hand, heirloom seeds (the term *heirloom* was popularized in 1981 by Kent Whealy of the Seed Savers Exchange) produce fruit with seeds that are just like the seeds that grew them. As the name suggests, heirloom seeds have been passed from generation to generation, farmer to farmer, and gardener to gardener, because they're tasty or have other desirable traits.

The Seed Savers Exchange sells seeds for vegetables I've never seen. If a grocery store is a suburban-mall pet shop, the Seed Savers Exchange is an exotic-animal bazaar. The melons shown on its Web site look like alien food props from an episode of the original *Star Trek*. I ordered a packet of Banana Melon seeds (twenty-five for $2.75) based on the fruit's unusual shape and color. From the catalogue description:

> *According to the Cucurbits of New York, this variety has been listed as a novelty for as long as American seed catalogs have been in print. Long banana-shaped melon tapered at both ends, 16–24" by 4" diameter. Smooth yellow skin, salmon-pink flesh. Good sweet spicy flavor.*

In addition to the Banana Melons, I bought seeds for several kinds of tomatoes—Cream Sausage, Bloody Butcher, Hillbilly Potato Leaf, Cherokee Purple, Crnkovic Yugoslavian—plus Miniature Chocolate bell peppers, sunberries, Aunt Molly's ground cherries, summer crookneck squash, A & C pickling cucumbers, Chioggia beets, Dragon carrots, Empress beans. I also bought a mixture of lettuces: Amish Deer Tongue, Australian Yellow-leaf, Bronze Arrowhead, Forellenschuss, Lolla Rossa, Pablo, Red Velvet, and Reine des Glaces. (I confess, I bought most of these seeds based more on their whimsical names than on their physical attributes.)

Even though the Home Depot tomatoes had been a bust, other vegetable plants (from seeds bought at the supermarket) were supplying us with a tidy harvest of cayenne peppers, figs, basil, squash, tomatoes, and watermelon. By midsummer, the average weekly haul was about ten or fifteen pounds of produce (not including oranges and grapefruits).

My garden produce looked so good that I often picked it and ate it without first going inside to wash it off. One afternoon I ate several figs, tomatoes, and basil leaves right off the plants, cleaning them by wiping them on my T-shirt.

That evening, as we were getting ready for bed, my stomach was feeling bloated and rumbly. I asked Carla how she felt, and she said she was fine. I figured my stomach discomfort was from eating three large bowls of the delicious homegrown-squash soup I'd made that afternoon. After falling into a light, restless sleep, I woke up at one-thirty in the morning with a sharp pain that started in the pit of my stomach and went all the way up to my esophagus. The pain rose and fell in waves, never going away completely, just cycling between "bad" and "excruciating." I felt hot and nauseated, and my abdomen was swollen. I got up and started walking around the house to alleviate my suffering (moving around felt better than lying in bed). I stayed up most of the night.

At around 5 a.m. I crawled into bed, feeling more miserable than before. For the entire day, I lay motionless, not eating or drinking, getting out of bed only to throw up or deal with a bout of diarrhea. I'd been cocky about the recent *E. coli* and salmonella breakouts in commercially grown produce, boasting to everyone within earshot that homegrown produce wasn't contaminated with pathogens. But my pesticide-free produce was undoubtedly crawling with microbes.

Fortunately it was just a twenty-four-hour bug, and by that evening the gastrointestinal distress had passed. But it had lasted long enough to teach me to always wash my produce before eating it.

When I related my experience to a coworker via e-mail, she told me about a friend, an industrial hygienist who diagnoses "sick buildings" for fungus infestation and has become something of a germophobe:

> She was picking raspberries from my yard and dropped some on the ground—she took them home and washed them with a (very) mild bleach solution before she ate them. She poohpoohs (heh) a lot of mold concerns, but she says the ground is crawling with E. coli type stuff. From raccoon and possum and rodent poo. Ew.

That seemed like overkill to me. But I still carefully wash my homegrown produce (without bleach).

## "WE HAVE GOPHER NEUROMANCERS"

My small garden was producing a fair amount of vegetables. By September I was the proud owner of a sizable plot of land formerly known as a lawn, and I was ready to take my gardening to the next level. First, though, I needed advice from someone who was already doing what I was thinking about doing, so I visited the home of Julian Darley and Celine Rich in Sebastopol, California. They're the founders of the Post Carbon Institute, a nonprofit organization established to figure out how people might be able to live reasonably well in a world without cheap energy.

When I arrived at their house at about ten o'clock in the morning, Julian, a sandy-haired Englishman around fifty, was standing in his driveway inspecting a new scratch in one of his "solar share" vehicles—pickups run on batteries charged by the rows of photovoltaic cells on the roof of the house.

Running his finger over the scratch, Julian asked out loud to no one in particular, "I wonder if this was intentional?" He called his wife, Celine, a pretty blond Canadian, to have a look. She shrugged noncommittally.

As Julian continued to examine the scratch, my eyes wandered to the enormous variety of fruits, vegetables, herbs, and grains growing on every square foot of the one-third-acre property. I saw an explosion of squash, sorghum, buckwheat, beans, corn, amaranth, mustard, soybeans, sunflowers, pumpkins, watermelons, lettuces, tomatoes, flax, hops, peppers, eggplants, okra, green peppers, basil, onions, and kiwi fruit. An irrigation system built from conduits and tiny ponds wound through the yard. Eighteenth-century farm implements were lined up against a shack. I was overwhelmed by how much stuff was growing, and by the thought of how much planning and work must have gone into making a garden this productive.

Julian noticed me staring at the garden. "It's gone a bit wild," he said. "There are a *lot* of ideas in here. We're not expecting anybody to *do* this but to take some of the ideas that you find appropriate and then turn them into your own garden for the minimum spend—minimum petroleum, minimum money."

Forgetting about the scratch on his car, Julian led me around the yard. "We've tried *many* different things that you can see, and now we're really homing in on"—and here his voice dropped to an urgent whisper—"*how you can do it cheaply.*"

"I'm interested in learning how to garden more cheaply," I said. "I paid a lot for my mulch. Is all this hay you're using for mulch cheaper?"

"That is straw," Julian said. "Hay is a feedstuff and would attract unwelcome critters. Besides, straw *is* cheaper."

The problem, though, he said, is that straw must be delivered by truck, and that just won't be practical in the post-carbon world, where gasoline costs a hundred dollars or more a gallon.

"Where does the straw come from?" he asked rhetorically. "It comes from the Midwest. It's a complete *energy loser.* It's crazy."

I quickly learned that, to Julian and Celine, DIY is a matter of mankind's survival, because they are certain we will be living in a post-carbon world in a couple of decades. But they don't rule out the personal-fulfillment angle—Julian describes his work as "serious with a smile."

Everything that takes place in the Post Carbon Institute's experimental garden and workshop is entered into an EROEI—energy return on energy invested—equation. In other words, how much energy (food calories, electric watts, thermal BTUs, etc.) are you getting out of an activity relative to how much energy it takes?

Julian brushed aside some of the straw with one foot to show me the white plastic conduits hiding beneath it. The water pipes led to green plastic boxes buried in the ground. Inside these boxes were the valves and filters for the irrigation system. Julian lifted the lid on a box to show me, but it was filled with so much dirt that I couldn't see much of anything.

"This is what the gophers do," he said of the mess. The gophers even ate through a plastic bag to get to the printed instructions stored in one of the boxes. "The little devils!" Julian said, holding the dirty plastic bag at eye level so he could get a better look. "The instructions are all going moldy."

Gophers are a big problem for gardeners everywhere, but in

this hippy-dippy northern California town, the solutions tend to be idiosyncratic. "People meditate to get rid of gophers," said Julian. "We have gopher neuromancers. Everybody has a story or a solution. The stories are interesting, and the solutions don't work."

"We have a big gopher problem," agreed Celine. She handed me an eight-inch-long black plastic cylinder with a pointed tip. It looked like some kind of dangerous sex toy. "You put this in the ground, and it makes noise to scare the gophers away." She turned it on, and it emitted an abrasive tone, like a digital alarm clock. "The problem is, it doesn't last. It runs a week or two, making that sound every minute or so, but once you put it in the ground, it stops working. I put it in strategic spots I know they like—the onion and cabbage patch and the watermelons. Then they all stopped working and the gophers all came back."

Julian said the batteries were fine, but he suspects the problem comes from bad contacts. "This stuff has to be much more *robust,*" he said. Anything not robust in the post-carbon age is going to be useless.

Julian showed me the computer that controls the irrigation system. It's about the size of a paperback book, with buttons to program the watering schedule. The gophers haven't gotten to it yet. It uses expensive, nonrechargeable eighteen-volt batteries. "Rechargeable batteries aren't practical," said Julian, "unless you are willing to change them out once a week." Julian and Celine's goal is to power the system with solar energy, which is "the trick with *all* this stuff."

They're also growing castor beans, which they are thinking about using to poison the gophers. (Castor beans contain ricin, a poisonous protein. A spy in London carried a James Bond–like umbrella that surreptitiously and fatally shot a tiny ricin-filled pellet into the leg of a journalist in 1978.) "We are trying to figure out if we can grind up the pods and then put them down the gopher holes," said Celine. "Or maybe we grow them in different places in the garden, because the roots are poisonous as well, but I'm not sure. Harvesting them will be my next challenge."

Julian nodded at the word *challenge*. "We find that at some stage in the process you get stuck. You get short of knowledge, short of time, you don't know what to do with it, you're missing the tools, blah blah blah. When you do a garden this complex, there are a lot of things to go wrong." It was nice to hear that other people experienced problems with their gardens, too.

Celine started picking vegetables for our lunch. She came across some sorghum and handed me a sprig. A couple of days before my visit, they had harvested their sorghum crop, which had grown to a height of twelve feet, and were able to extract five gallons of the sweet, calorie-rich juice using a hundred-year-old cast-iron sorghum press.

The more time I spent with Julian and Celine, the more I respected them. They weren't blindly optimistic about going back to the land. Instead, they approached the problem as amateur scientists, using their garden and workshop as a laboratory to test tools and technologies that might help people live in a world without cheap energy. They are hopeful about solar and wind energy, but their outlook on biofuels, which many green-energy enthusiasts promote, is gloomy. Celine and Julian have tried extracting oil from energy crops such as sunflower, flax, and canola seeds without success. They've used a variety of hand presses (because a gas or electric press would be cheating), and none are strong enough to squeeze oil from the tiny seeds. "We haven't managed to squish anything," said Julian. He held out some canola seeds, and I was surprised to see how minuscule and hard-shelled they looked. Julian said he brings canola seeds with him when he goes to conventions to show them to biodiesel boosters, "and their jaws literally drop."

"A lot of what we try to do," he said, "is explore this food-versus-fuel debate, and the crude conclusion is that liquid fuels are very hard to make, so you should treat them very preciously." In fact, according to Post Carbon Institute fellow Rob Hopkins, a liter of petroleum "contains the energy equivalent of about five weeks hard human manual labor." At $3 a gallon, Julian pointed out, gasoline is an unbelievable bargain. When we run out of gasoline and can't use gas-powered farm equipment, we'll need other sources of fuel to produce the food we eat. Julian and Celine built this garden to try as many different human-, wind-, and solar-powered methods as they could think of before the oil runs out.

They also grew flax seeds, which they were initially excited about because the seeds provide omega-3 oil and the plant is the source of linen. But it turns out that making linen requires a number of skills and machines. Flax has to be retted, scutched, hackled, spun, reeled, woven, bleached, and dyed to become linen. For the self-sufficiency purist, flax isn't practical. But, as Julian pointed out, a local community composed of skilled tradespeople could convert flax into linen. Flax, it turns out, is a DIO—do-it-ourselves—material.

Julian had just started telling me about last year's basil harvest ("a sea of green and purple leaves") when an older woman walking on the sidewalk stopped in front of the gate leading to their house and shouted to Julian and Celine, "Guys, is it no on seven?"

She was asking about California Proposition 7, a state measure that had been heavily advertised as an alternative-energy plan that would cut the state's reliance on fossil fuels.

"No on 7," said Julian. "No on 7, no on 10, yes on 1A—that's the railway."

"Why no on 7?" asked the woman. "To me, it's—"

Julian cut her off. "Because it's another *fiddle*. It's two Arizona *billionaires* trying to foist basically Big Solar, which won't help Small Solar. The Small Solar people *hate* it."

Julian and Celine are against the big guy and for the little guy, not because they have some kind of ideological dislike of large corporations but simply because they don't think large, centralized suppliers of food, energy, and manufactured goods will be viable when the oil runs out. (In a 2009 talk at the annual TED conference, Rob Hopkins explained that for every four barrels of oil we use, only one new barrel is discovered.) When the pumps go dry, the people who survive will be the ones who are parts of local communities that have figured out how to generate their own electricity and share it with their neighbors. "Our motto," said Julian, "is reduce consumption and produce locally."

I press Julian on why Big Solar is bad. Isn't it better than coal?

"Big Solar means long transmission lines, to Los Angeles, San Diego, and so forth," he explained. "They are expensive, and you have losses, and so our theme is 'Shorten the supply chains.' Do it as locally as you can. Try to trim your consumption to match your local supply. No doubt we'll need big sources, but that's not what we try to promote. We promote what ordinary people can do, what towns can do, what regions can do."

I also learned that coffee and tea won't be around in the post-carbon world. "If you look at the embedded energy of the things people eat and drink," said Celine, "coffee and tea are really big. And even if it's fair trade, those people are concentrating on growing things for the export market rather than helping to make their families self-reliant and growing the staple crops of their community. Now if you're a Somalian, I could see that growing coffee would be a staple crop, but I don't think that's a traditional Vietnamese staple crop. *They* need to be growing crops that will be feeding *their* communities, and *we* need to be growing crops that will feed *our* communities."

To show me an example of what she means by feeding her community, Celine led me to the front porch, where there was a table with a weighing scale and a notebook and pen. There was also a chalkboard with produce prices written on it. This is Celine's "you pick" program for selling the produce grown in the energy garden. Four or five families in the neighborhood come over and pick fruits, vegetables, and eggs from the garden. They weigh the fruit on a scale on the front porch and write down the type of produce they picked and how much it weighed in a notebook. Later, Celine collects the money. She charges the same prices that the farmers' market in town charges: Basil is $2 a bunch, squash cost 50 cents each, tomatoes are $2 a handful, and eggs are $4 a dozen.

I asked Julian and Celine which activity yields the highest energy return on energy invested. Celine pointed to the fifteen hens scratching around in the straw mulch, looking for bugs to eat.

"We looked at the energy output of the garden, and we figured out that most of it is coming from eggs," she said.

"About ten chickens equals one human in terms of calorie needs," added Julian. "They need about two hundred calories per day, and they output about one hundred calories in eggs in the summer. That's pretty generous."

"If you compost a lot," said Celine, "that builds up the insects, and you get even better eggs. They make the eggs really high in the right kind of omega-3 fatty acids as opposed to eggs from hens fed a corn diet."

Julian added that the neighbors have been bringing food scraps over to feed the hens. For now, the neighbors give them the scraps out of the kindness of their hearts, but Julian plans on eventually paying them in solars (rhymes with *dollars*), a local currency backed up by units of solar energy. "We haven't done it yet," he said, "because we want to make sure the mechanism's right."

Near the back of the property, I saw different kinds of equipment. The worm composter had been knocked over in a recent storm, but it still contained a large mass of wriggling worms. The worms, said Celine, eat garbage and excrete a "tea," which is a powerful fertilizer that she sprinkles on plants.

Near the composter sat the remains of a large alcohol still made from a fifty-five-gallon drum. It wasn't meant for making moonshine but, rather, for converting waste fruit into alcohol for fuel. "It's not so easy to do, as it turns out," said Julian. "Let's just say we haven't mastered it."

"Why not?" I asked.

"You have to know what you're doing much better than we did," said Julian. "There's a lot of skill involved in a lot of this stuff."

Feeling overwhelmed, I reminded myself that Julian and Celine were approaching gardening from a different perspective than most gardeners. They wanted to learn how people could survive in a post-carbon world, a world where machinery to make juice from apples, bottles to hold the juice, and refrigeration to keep the juice fresh—anything that required remotely manufactured equipment or fossil fuels—were out of the question.

I could appreciate where they were coming from, but my reasons for gardening and preserving food were different. To me, making apple juice was an excuse to get a nifty apple press and learn how it worked, and to design labels to put on bottles of juice for friends. Yes, Julian and Celine were being more practical about the future of the human race, but I didn't want to go there. I was interested in gardening *because* of the challenges.

## RAMSHACKLE SOLID

I learned a lot from Julian and Celine, but I felt I needed to learn from folks who were operating on a wavelength closer to mine.

I recalled a visit I'd made in late June with Mister Jalopy's old friends Eric Thomason and Julia Posey, who run a blog about their urban-homesteading adventure called Ramshackle Solid. Mister Jalopy explained that if I was interested in DIY living, I owed it to myself to get to know them. From their 1926 house (likely built as a cabin for hunters when grizzly bears roamed the hills between Los Angeles and Pasadena), Eric and Julia and their two small kids have been experimenting with gardening, composting, crafting, sewing, growing native plants, cooking and baking and slow food, amateur entomology, beekeeping, and foraging—a life they sum up as "ramshackle solid." Julia works part time as a reporter for a public radio station in Pasadena. Eric is an artist and a designer for Yahoo.

Eric and Julia invited me to their house, on a hill behind a gate guarded by two big pit bull mixes, which turned out to be a couple of marshmallows. Eric—tall, thin, with a couple of days' growth of beard—shushed the dogs and let me through the gate. I ran my eyes over the property and decided that *ramshackle* was an apt word to describe it. An ancient flatbed pickup truck that obviously didn't run sat in the yard between two outbuildings, one of which was starting to sink because the asphalt driveway was slowly caving in. "The shack is made out of old doors," said Eric. "It's what they call farmhouse construction, where there are no two-by-fours. The whole wall is just one-by-twelves. I don't even know how they built it. I think they framed it on the ground and then tipped it up and nailed it together, like at a barn raising. There are no vertical beams and no roof beam. Whenever somebody who knows something about construction comes in and looks at it, they say, 'How's this thing even standing?'" He pointed up to the main residence. "The whole house is built that way, too."

I noticed small mounds of fresh dirt around the property. Like Julian and Celine, the Ramshackle Solid homestead had a gopher.

It had been wreaking havoc on the root vegetables for the past three months, Eric told me.

Picking up an acorn and gesturing to the tree above us, he said, "That oak is huge, and it's got a ton of acorns in it."

"Can you eat them?" I asked.

"We did last year. It's really cool. You can get a really nutty, coarse flour, and you can mix it into pancakes. The buckwheat is also really good," he said, pointing to a patch of pinkish flowers. "What you do is get the whole flowers and save them in a bag. You can mix them with a little bit of Bisquick and make buckwheat biscuits. They're almost black, and they're really perfumey. They're good with honey."

The property is covered with native California holly, from which Hollywood got its name. Also known as toyon, the shrubs are about eight feet tall and have reddish berries. "It makes such killer compost," Eric said. "If I trim the leaves and mulch them, they'll compost in three months easily. I go around and look for things that need a bit of pruning. I get the stuff together, run it through the mulcher, and end up with an almost perfect mix of dry and green that'll cook up really, really hot."

He led me over to the compost pile. I picked up a handful of compost—it looked like crumbly chocolate cake and had a clean earth smell. "It's even got a red wiggler in it," said Eric, pointing out a worm. "And there's a worm egg." The egg was surprisingly large.

"I planted that little orange tree over there," Eric said. "It was diseased and curled up and had bugs on it. I was reading about organic gardening and read that the plants will get diseased if you don't have good soil—so I just took some of this stuff and dumped it around the base of the tree, in the old wagon-wheel rim that I put around it. I filled it with compost and put mulch on top of it and watered it. Immediately it just grew like crazy. Two days later it had like four inches of growth on every branch."

"You didn't have to dig down to the roots to get the compost into the tree?" I asked.

"The water sent down the loam—that superfine silky stuff with the micronutrients in it. It just went crazy. Now it's got about two feet on it."

We headed into the main house and went into the kitchen, where Julia was making muffins and brewing coffee. It smelled wonderful.

Eric poured everyone a cup of coffee, and we settled in the living room. I asked them what they are trying to accomplish with their foray into ramshackle living.

"We're still trying to figure out exactly what the motivation is for the decisions we're making," Eric admitted. "There's an aspect of imperfection in the stuff we're doing—that's part of the name Ramshackle Solid. I like imperfection. I like something that's been reworked or modified in an unintended direction and the way that that shapes the outcome of the project. It seems to have more of a . . ." and here he paused, searching for the right word. "It seems more *real*. It seems more like it's a living thing or has a history at that point. If everything's perfect, it's kind of boring. And if there are modifications that have to be made or adjustments or things like that, they give it character and interest, and also somehow they add meaning."

Eric offered the example of fixing a hinged trash-can lid. "I'm on my fourth attempt," he said. "I tried to fix it with wire. It held together for a week. Then I got these pieces of galvanized metal, and I made little hoops and used a finishing nail for a hinge. But it wouldn't stay on, so I taped it on, just because I wanted to be done with it, and it held for like six months. Recently I soldered it, and now I have these two rods, which is where I ended up. I'm happy with all aspects of it. I'm happy that it works now, but it's not just about it working; somehow it's about arriving at the solution, the trial and error. I probably never would have come up with that solution in the first place. Or, if I'd really thought about it and not been kind of half-assed the whole time, I probably would have gone to the store and bought something that's the right piece that could screw on the end and had a hinge and maybe a bolt or rivet that let the hinge move. But it wouldn't be as interesting as what I have now. And I also have the history that evolves with it. Every time I open that trash can now, I have a little sense of satisfaction over how it opens. I never noticed the trash can opening before."

Eric's experience with the trash-can lid is something I've heard over and over again from DIYers. They thrive on constantly challenging themselves to learn how to make things and fix things on their own. It's an appealing alternative to buying solutions to every problem that arises. Eric invented his own solution and, as a result, he feels a connection to the trash-can lid and cares about it. In a culture where everything is built to be disposed of at the first sign of trouble, it's harder to care about or even be aware of the objects in your life. But when you become personally invested in the care and maintenance of something, you appreciate it more. I notice this myself with the plants in our yard. I don't really care what happens to the plants that I didn't put in the ground myself, but I *am* interested in the well-being of the ones that I did, because they embody my time and effort.

It started getting warm in the living room, so we moved out to the big canvas tent Eric and Julia had erected on a deck to drink our coffee and continue our conversation. The tent was open on three sides, shady and breezy.

I asked them how far they wanted to go down the road of self-sufficiency. "We would love to be able to grow all our own food and be totally self-sustaining," said Eric. "But it's also about creating a place for the kids. It's also about buying stuff only when we need to. It's about making more of everything we need—not just garden stuff but making shelves instead of buying them from Ikea, or creating systems that work, like an organization system."

"Why is it important for you to be able to do that?"

"It feels like it's about creating a lifestyle that's more rewarding," Eric replied. "It's about breaking from that consumer cycle and living a more natural life. Over the last hundred years we've gotten so far from that. I think it's detrimental to society and individuals. I think it's about trying to reconnect, not just with the land but with a more sane and sustainable way to live. Not just ecological sustainability but a sustainable way to live with the daily rituals you perform and a lifestyle that works better. For me anyway."

— — — — — — — — —

Eric and Julia invited me back to their house in November. They wanted to show off the shack they'd built on the slope of their property, which Eric was going to use as his painting studio. They'd also invited Mister Jalopy, and Erik Knutzen and Kelly Coyne of the Homegrown Evolution blog, to come along.

Before driving to their place, I took care of a few chores around the house. I fed and watered our chickens, who were a few weeks old at that point. In addition to the chick starter mash they'd been eating, I fed them some of the green flowering buds on my basil plants. The chicks seemed to enjoy the change of diet. I also found some day-old pancakes in the refrigerator, so Sarina and I brought them to the coop to see if the chickens would be interested in eating them. They didn't like it when we held a pancake out to them, but when we crumbled one up in a pan, they went crazy for it. When one of the chickens snatched a piece, she'd run to a corner and the other chickens would chase her, grabbing the morsel out of her beak. They'd fight for a while over the crumb, ignoring the bounty in the pan.

Back in the garden, I collected the dried flowers on the basil plants, and Jane and I rubbed them between our fingers over a bowl to collect the tiny black seeds and save them in an envelope so we could plant them next spring.

In the kitchen, I rotated the trays of persimmons that I was drying and then went into the yard to collect the pineapple guavas that had fallen off the tree. Jane and I shared a few. I was surprised that she liked the tart, exotic flavor of the guavas (also known as feijoas), because I'd thought of her as a picky eater. Strangely, she wanted nothing to do with the dried persimmons, which are as sweet and as mild as taffy.

The morning was still cool, so I went to the garden to plant lettuce seeds I'd ordered from the Seed Saver's Exchange and garlic bulbs I'd picked up at a nursery near my house. The bag contained three garlic bulbs, and the label clearly showed the entire bulb being planted in the ground with the instructions, "Place bulbs in hole, pointed ends up." I dug three holes to the indicated depth, spaced five inches apart from one another, and put one bulb in each hole.

I planted another couple of rows of lettuce before calling it quits for the morning. I had to wash up and get ready for lunch at Ramshackle Solid. Carla had other plans that day, so I brought Jane and Sarina with me. I filled a bag with persimmons and feijoas to give to Eric and Julia and drove over to their place. I parked my car near the chain-link gate in front of the house. As we approached, their two pit bull mutts barked excitedly. Jane scrambled into my arms, and Sarina hid behind me. Jane said she didn't want to go in. But Mister Jalopy's wife, Lynette, appeared and assured the girls that the dogs were simply happy to meet new visitors. Mrs. Jalopy led us to a wooden gate, and the dogs trotted up to us, wagging their tails.

Parked in the driveway was a dilapidated Airstream trailer that hadn't been there the last time I'd visited. We went inside to find Mister Jalopy having a conversation with Julia and Eric's four-year-old son, Emmet. Somehow he had managed to climb into a cubbyhole about four feet off the floor. It was hot inside the trailer. The built-in cabinetry was distressed, windows were broken, and fixtures were missing. Eric's friend, a thin, intense, quiet man named Phoenix, had been spending the weekend stripping the paint from the aluminum interior walls with a variety of volatile solvents, which were lined up on a counter in the trailer's kitchen. I started feeling queasy from inhaling those toxic chemicals inside the stuffy enclosure.

I shepherded my kids outside to find Julia and Lynette bringing out lunch, a smorgasbord of homemade dishes prepared from produce grown on the property. Julia had baked bread, and Sarina helped herself to two pieces. Erik and Kelly had brought humongous pink and yellow tomatoes, sliced into discs roughly the size of 45 rpm records.

Jane wasn't hungry, so she and Emmet climbed in a tree while the adults ate and talked about everything from the recent presidential-election results to homesteading tips. I asked Erik and Julia what vegetables were good to grow in the winter and when I could expect my hens (which were about four or five weeks old) to start laying eggs and how long they'd reliably lay them.

When I mentioned that I'd planted garlic earlier in the morning, Kelly said she usually waits until Thanksgiving to plant hers but that it was probably fine to plant the cloves now.

"You can plant individual garlic *cloves*?" I asked. "I planted the whole bulb."

Kelly explained that you were supposed to break apart a bulb and plant the cloves. What's more, she told me, I could have used inexpensive garlic from the grocery store or farmers' market instead of buying the bulbs from a nursery. I told them how the instructions clearly showed and stated that the entire bulb should be planted. Mister Jalopy got a good chuckle out of that.

"You plant three bulbs and you get three bulbs," he observed.

After lunch, we took a look at the shack Eric and Phoenix had built on the side of the hill. They'd based the design on a photo I'd come across online a few months earlier of architect Jeffery Broadhurst's shack, a little getaway retreat he'd built in the hills of West Virginia. Erected on stilts, with a single sloped tin roof and wide doors opening onto a small deck, the simple structure was cheerful and airy. I could imagine myself spending hours of every day in a shack like this one.

Julia told me that they'd been thinking of building a zip line that would go from the shack all the way to the garden down at the bottom of the property, but now the trailer was blocking the route.

When we got home from our day at the Ramshackle compound, I made dinner with more of our garden's vegetables. I crushed the shells of the eggs we'd eaten earlier to feed to the chickens, then I chopped up a head of cabbage, added salt, and put it in a quart-sized mason jar to turn into sauerkraut. Sarina told me she liked the Ramshackle shack and said she had been scoping out the trees in our yard for zip lines and treehouses. When we were finished eating, she led me around the yard, explaining the pros and cons of the different trees. That evening Jane, Sarina, and I sat down and went through several treehouse books written by David Stiles, regarded by many as the king of treehouse architecture. We highlighted our favorites with Post-it notes.

I was just a few months into my DIY life experiment, and already I felt more connected to what I ate, the property around my house, the cycles of the seasons, the neighbors who shared my interests, and best of all my kids.

# THE WORLD ACCORDING TO ALFIE

It wasn't always so blissfully DIY at our place. Many a day would pass when my family would eat fast food and watch lots of DVDs and play hours of video games, or I'd sit in front of my computer all day, working to the exclusion of everything else. I started to feel guilty about not doing enough on my DIY to-do list. Sometimes I'd rush things, like preparing a bowl of persimmons for drying or tending to the chickens. Hurrying took all the fun out of it. So I came up with a plan to schedule a little time every day to work on a project and made a promise to myself to slow down and remain mindful of the task for twenty minutes. I'd use that bit of time to accomplish a small project, like pulling weeds in the garden or making a new batch of kombucha tea (a fizzy, tangy, fermented brew made from water, sugar, and black tea), or to complete one step in a larger project, like sawing fret grooves in the neck of a cigar-box guitar or building a miniature guitar amplifier.

These DIY mini-sessions were refreshing breaks from blogging, editing, and writing, and the twenty-minute sessions really added up! I made my fifth cigar-box guitar this way, in twenty-minute increments. I was reminded of the seventeenth-century French chancellor Henri-François d'Aguesseau, who wrote a best-selling, three-volume book ten minutes at a time while waiting for his habitually late wife to join him at the dinner table.

One early December afternoon in 2008, while I was working in my office in the guesthouse, I heard a car honking loudly outside. I knew it wasn't the UPS guy, because he always announced his arrival with two polite taps on his truck horn. This honking sounded urgent. I hurried out of the cottage and saw a dust-covered brown 1980s Crown Victoria in the driveway. When I got closer, I recognized the driver. It was Alfie.

Alfie's a short, sturdy man who looks like Picasso. He's about eighty years old. We first met one morning about four years ago, when I went outside to pick figs from our tree. Alfie was already there, picking figs and putting them into a paper bag. He saw me, said hello, and kept picking. His audaciousness irked me. I curtly told him to save some of the figs for me; I was the tree's owner, after all.

"But they're rotting!" he exclaimed. I saw that one of his eyes was bright blue, the other milky white.

"I don't care," I said. "I don't want you to take any more."

He grumbled and got into his car and drove off, taking several pounds of my figs with him. I picked the remaining ripe figs off the tree and brought them into the house. I had just started to tell Carla what had happened when we heard an insistent series of honks outside. I looked out the window.

"That's him!" I told Carla. "He came back!"

"Go out and see what he wants."

I met Alfie as he was getting out of his car. In his hands were a plastic bag and a small knife with an orange handle.

"I want to give you this," he said, handing the bag to me. It was filled with garden-grown peppers, parsley, and basil. "And look at this," he said. He leaned into the open window of his car and grabbed a page from an Arabic newspaper. "Now, watch." He held a corner of the sheet of newspaper in one hand and, with the orange-handled knife in his other hand, began slicing strips from the newspaper, letting them fall to the ground.

"These are my knives," he said. "They can slice anything— except *raw meat*. Cooked meat, OK, raw meat—don't do it. My knives are in all the Subways. They all know me! Tell them you know Alfie. This knife is for you." He held the knife out to me, handle side first.

Sheepishly I took the knife and introduced myself. I apologized for getting crabby with him about the figs. He explained that the previous owners of our house had given him permission to harvest figs and persimmons from the property, and he hadn't realized they'd moved. I told him he was welcome to take our figs anytime, and he thanked me.

"Follow me," he said. He got in his car and started driving away very slowly. I walked quickly behind the car to keep up. I wondered how long I was going to have to follow him down the street, and where we were going.

Alfie turned the corner and drove very slowly for another half a block, stopping in front of a vacant lot barricaded by a metal fence. He got out and unlocked the gate. The lot was about a half acre and was filled with black five-gallon plastic containers holding pepper bushes, citrus trees, and more. There were numerous other vegetables growing in the ground, along with dozens of trees sagging with fruit.

"This was my house," he said. "It was destroyed in the earthquake." (He was referring to the Northridge earthquake of 1994, which killed fifty-seven people, injured at least nine thousand people, and caused between $20 billion to $40 billion in damage.) Alfie's house had been beyond repair, so he'd torn it down and turned it into a very large garden. He lived with his wife in a condominium a couple of miles away.

I wasn't as interested in gardening then as I am now, so I didn't give too much thought to his garden, nor did I ask many questions about his methods for producing such bumper crops.

As the months passed, Alfie's honks (and gifts of knives) became a welcome and almost regular occurrence. I started paying more attention to the tips he offered. He told me I should collect fallen leaves and lawn clippings into a pile near my garden to make compost. He explained how to prune away the branches from the fig tree once growing season was over to ensure a good harvest the following year. Usually he offered this advice while helping himself to our persimmons, loquats, and feijoas, always without asking. By this time, I liked Alfie too much to care about this quirk of his. He never went into much detail about himself, but I learned that he was from Iran and that, besides being a knife salesman, he had also been in the book-distribution business.

I hadn't seen Alfie for a few months, and I was happy to see him that day in December. He'd brought his wife along, a pretty, well-dressed woman who looked to be ten or fifteen years his junior.

"Do you remember me?" he asked.

"Of course I do, Alfie!" I said, opening the gate to let them in.

"Good!" he replied. "I've been trying to come here for persimmons, but you aren't home."

"I guess we just missed each other." I told him that all the persimmons were already off the tree but that I'd dried a bunch. I went in the house to get some for him. When I stepped back outside, Alfie was shaking the branches of the feijoa tree to make the fruits drop to the ground. He had about six of them in his hands, so I went back inside to get a bag for him, for which he thanked me. He filled the bag with fruit, went to his car, and gave me another knife, demonstrating its sharpness on a sheet of newspaper.

"Do you want to come with me now?" he asked. "I have things to give you." I was interested to find out how his garden was coming along in the late fall. I hopped on my bicycle and pedaled behind his car.

Once we had arrived at the yard, Alfie and his wife got out of the car, and Alfie's wife settled in one of the plastic lawn chairs under a large tree.

"One day, I come over, I give your wife recipes," said Alfie. "If you eat, you go crazy. You say, 'I live so long, I never tasted this food?' Something out of this world. You're going to thank me all your life."

Alfie's wife told me to bring my bike into the lot so no one would take it.

"Good idea," I said, then brought it into the yard and leaned it against a tree.

"Where did you learn to cook?" I asked Alfie.

"Oh, I know a lot of good recipes," he said, leading me through the rain-soaked garden. "I know Israeli food, I know Iraqi food, I know Persian food. I know things you could not even imagine."

Birds squawked at us from the trees.

"Everything is mutual," he said. "If you're nice to me, I'm nice to you. I like you. The first time I met you I thought you were a good person." (I wondered how he could think that after I'd acted so peevish about his fig pilfering.)

He led me to the back of the lot. There were so many trees and tall plants around that I felt like I was in another country, not a mere block away from my house. A rooster crowed off in the distance.

"I will show you something," he said.

Alfie stopped in front of a plant loaded with chubby little green peppers. He picked one and handed it to me. "Eat this. It's clean. Eat this pepper. It's sweet." I popped it into my mouth. He was right. It was sweet and crunchy. "It's like cucumber," he said.

"What kind of pepper is it? What's it called?"

Ignoring my question, he said, "I show you here." He picked up a one-gallon plastic container with a pepper plant, pulled a few of the brown leaves, and handed the pot to me. "Here. I give you this one."

I thanked him and asked him again what kind of pepper it was.

"No, no. This is different. You don't find this in America."

"Where did you get them?"

He turned away from me. "From Middle East, I get." He

started picking peppers from the larger bushes and handing them to me. I had no bag, so I stuffed them in my pockets. "They usually sweet at this stage, but be careful, because the weather is changing."

I tried one. "They're sweet," I said.

"If you pick them small, they are sweet," he said. "And I give you some recipes how you can use." He started off in a new direction. I followed.

I noticed a run-down chicken coop along a fence near the back. "Did you keep chickens here?"

"I did keep, but a dog came and killed them." He stopped in front of a large pile of black compost, surrounded by ten or twelve five-gallon plastic pots full of the stuff in various stages of decomposition.

"This is the best compost in the world, because this has worms."

"Did you put worms in it?" I asked, looking at the pink and red earthworms wriggling in the soil he was upturning in one of the containers.

"They create worms!" he said. I asked him what he meant by "create worms." He explained that crushed old fruit will spontaneously generate worms.

I had no desire to argue with him. I was more interested in finding out how he made this loamy compost.

"The scientists," he continued, "they even don't know how this worms eat the leaf and the shit that comes out of them—it's the best fertilizer in the world. Oh, my God, everything grow like you can't even imagine."

It was hard getting a straight answer out of Alfie, because he was always on to the next thing, walking away before I had a chance to fully understand something. But I told him I really wanted to know how he made the compost.

"I put leaves in a pile, and I put ammonium sulfate—you know ammonium sulfate? It looks like sugar. A bag twenty pounds for three dollars at Home Depot. Or horse manure. I mix and put water, and they will rot. They will be best fertilizer in the world. And something else—you know what is elephant garlic?"

"The giant garlic bulbs?"

"Yeah. I give you some babies, and if you grow them for thousands of years, without planting them every year you get some and they give babies and every year you will have them." I assumed he wasn't telling me to stick the garlic directly into the compost but just hopping from subject to subject a bit faster than technically comprehensible.

I was trying to memorize Alfie's compost recipe while he led me away. "I want you to try something else." We wound our way through the dense foliage. We passed by a fig tree, and I asked him about it.

"Oh, in March or February I give you cuttings. I have figs you've never tasted in your life. You don't see them in the market. I have four or five kinds. When you eat them—like chocolate. If you close your eyes and eat them, you think it's chocolate."

He stopped at a row of pepper plants and pulled a couple from each plant. Some were round like marbles, some were like small jalapeños, others were like cayennes. But they all tasted sweet. "You never get these peppers in America," he said again. "If you chop this and you put one or two hot also with them and make an omelet with eggs—ah, *delicious!*"

Since we were on the subject of food preparation, I asked him if he made his own yogurt.

"It's very easy. You know how?"

"No, I've been reading how to, but I don't really know."

"You boil the milk. It has to be whole milk. One or two boilings. Put it aside for a while until you can put finger in and it doesn't burn. Then you put one or two or three spoons of yogurt and mix it and cover it and put it in the oven for a little while without the oven on and you wait a little while."

Before I got the chance to ask him how long you have to wait, he had plucked a few small greenish-yellow fruits from a nearby tree. They looked like unripe grapefruits. "These fruits you've never tasted in all your life." He pulled a knife that was sticking blade down in a pot of dirt, rinsed it under a hose, and cut one of the lemons into quarters, handing it to me. I bit into it, expecting it to be tart, but it was just the opposite—sweet, like a kid's drink, without acidity.

"This is good!" I said. "Will it grow from a seed?" I was thinking of saving the seeds from the piece he'd given me.

"No. No."

"Is it something you got in the Middle East, too?"

"Yeah, yeah. And I'll tell about this. If somebody has cold, if you eat eight, ten of this, he's gonna jump back up after a day."

My pockets full of peppers and sweet lemons, I said goodbye to Alfie and his wife and rode my bike home.

– – – – – – – –

Since moving from Tarzana to Studio City in the spring of 2009, I have had to start over with a new garden. Unfortunately, the difficulty of the move and predator problems with the chickens have kept me too busy to establish the large garden I'd planned. And besides, the new property doesn't really offer a good gardening spot. I ended up buying several "Earth Boxes," plastic containers with a reservoir at the bottom that stores water, which wicks up into the soil, preventing it from drying out. The benefit of the system is that you don't have to water the plant every day, as you do with a normal container.

Earth Boxes come with a bag of soil and organic fertilizer. In early summer 2009, Jane and I transplanted some pepper, basil, and sunberry seedlings (from seeds I'd ordered the previous August) into them, and I was shocked at how fast the plants shot up. As our new deck is quite large, I could easily put twenty or more Earth Boxes on it and grow a bountiful fruit and vegetable harvest. But I won't grow sunberries again. They ripened and looked like delicious blueberries, but when Jane and I sampled them, they were loaded with hard, slimy seeds and had an offputting aftertaste. Jane was so disappointed in them that she almost cried. Fortunately, chickens love them.

I've also begun planting fruit trees, designating the steep undeveloped slope below the chicken coop as the orchard. I hope to establish fig, feijoa, grapefruit, citrus, and persimmon trees here, as we had at our place in Tarzana, as well as a variety of more exotic trees, such as dragonfruit, banana, pineapple, mango, cinnamon, and maybe even coffee, all of which have been successfully grown in Los Angeles. I'm sure it will take a long time for the trees to bear fruit, but I'm in no hurry.

Growing things to eat and making foods like yogurt, sauerkraut, and kombucha have only encouraged me to learn more, to try new gardening techniques, to preserve my harvests using different methods. When I meet a fellow food gardener, we end up talking endlessly about our experiments, failures, and successes. I can't think of anything more fascinating or engaging than the magic and science of converting tiny seeds into beautiful, tasty fruits and vegetables. I'm sorry I didn't start doing it earlier in life.

# 4 TICKLING MISS SILVIA

**"I define a Godshot as a better shot than I've ever made before. Each time I pull one, the bar goes up a little and it will be harder to pull the next one."**
**—KARL RICE, ALT.COFFEE NEWSGROUP, 2001, REFERRING TO THE PERFECT SHOT OF ESPRESSO**

Milanese manufacturing plant owner Luigi Bezzera was upset. In his opinion, his workers spent too much time making coffee and not enough time on his assembly lines. Bezzera devised a steam-powered solution to speed things up: a machine that shot steam through coffee grounds directly into a cup in just twenty seconds—coffee made to order. Now his employees could get their caffeine and get right back to work.

Bezzera's employees back in 1901 may not have appreciated their truncated breaks, but they loved the strong, caffeinated nectar. Figuring he was onto something, Bezzera patented his "fast coffee machine," now regarded as the first espresso machine. The coffee was somewhat bitter because the steam was too hot (higher temperatures produce bitter coffee, lower temperatures produce sour coffee), but it caught on. A few years later, Desiderio Pavoni bought Bezzera's patent and immediately went to work on improving it, the main modification being a pressure-relief valve. His

"Ideale" machine was introduced at the 1906 Milan International Fair, and while it was more successful than Bezzera's original, it still used the steam-extraction method that caused bitterness.

It wasn't until 1947, when Giovanni Achille Gaggia patented a machine with a lever-operated piston—doing away with the need for high-temperature steam to push water through the coffee— that modern espresso was born. In addition to producing a coffee that was less bitter and more acidic (not to be confused with sour- ness, acidity is something to be desired in coffee), Gaggia's inven- tion yielded a delicious new component: *crema,* the dark orange foam that forms on the top of a well-pulled shot of espresso.

Like millions of other people, I'm an espresso enthusiast. (The last time I can recall going without a cup of the black gold was in 1995, when I spent an otherwise fabulous day on an uninhabited island in the South Pacific.) Espresso is an important part of my life, a twice- (often thrice-) daily ritual for my wife and me. I'd been drink- ing coffee for years but never really appreciated it until, in my early twenties, I tried an espresso at a café in Denver. For the first time, I could really *taste* the coffee. That weak, sour brown water I'd been drinking during all-nighters in the dorm was nothing like this rich- smelling, strong drink that was served to me in a comically miniature cup with a slice of lemon peel on the side. The instant it passed my lips, I became hooked. I've made my own espresso for the past fifteen years or so, but despite having read many how-to articles, I never felt as though I'd gotten the hang of it. That started to bug me. If I was going to be drinking at least two double shots of espresso daily with- out fail, I decided I ought to get better at making my own.

The first thing I did was go online and read about making espresso. I discovered that there were a number of variables:

▶ The type of coffee bean (go for arabica, not robusta)
▶ The freshness of the roast (ideally, two weeks or less)

- ▶ The freshness of the grind (one day or less)
- ▶ The type of grind (burr, not blade)
- ▶ The amount of force used to tamp the coffee down in the filter (thirty pounds)
- ▶ The water temperature (198 degrees)
- ▶ The extraction time (twenty to thirty seconds)

Though I tried my best to control these variables, the appearance and taste of the espresso I made varied wildly from shot to shot. Sometimes the coffee gurgled out of the machine, weak and musty. Others, it dribbled out sour and muddy. Sometimes the grind was too fine, so the pump would choke on it, and only a few drops would come out.

But once in a while, my espresso was sublime, a rich layer of *crema* on top of a thick, strong shot of coffee. This kind of espresso, which tastes as good as roasted beans smell, is called a "Godshot" among professional and amateur baristas. The problem was, I had no idea why my espresso was heavenly some days, downright diabolical on others.

That's why, one Sunday morning in June 2008, I loaded my espresso machine and coffee grinder into the back of my car and drove to a gritty industrial neighborhood in East L.A. to meet the best espresso maker in the country.

Kyle Glanville greeted me at the R&D headquarters of Intelligentsia Coffee and Tea. Rail thin, with penetrating eyes and an Anthony Perkins haircut, he's perfectly cast for the role of "manager, espresso research and development." I had been buying Intelligentsia's Black Cat espresso beans by mail order for months. After seeing my favorable review of the beans on Boing Boing, Intelligentsia's marketing manager invited me to visit its new Los Angeles–based operation (the company started in Chicago). I jumped at the chance to polish my espresso-making skills.

Glanville shook my hand and welcomed me into the espresso testing room, a sparklingly clean laboratory with two industrial espresso machines and an array of grinders, thermometers, color charts, and glassware. Glanville had recently returned from Minneapolis, where he'd won first place at the Specialty Coffee Association of America's 2008 National Barista Championship. A panel of seven judges (four sensory, two technical, and one head judge) awarded Glanville top marks against the forty-nine other state champions for the taste and consistency of his espresso beverages, the creativity and style of his visual and verbal presentation, cleanliness, and demonstrated technical knowledge and skill.

I was taken on a tour of the facility. Behind the testing room is a rebuilt and upgraded fifty-year-old German coffee roaster with a cast-iron drum (which distributes heat evenly to the beans roasting inside). Off to the side were dozens of stacks of burlap bags filled with unroasted coffee beans. I grabbed a nearby scooper and scooped green beans from an opened sack. They had no smell as far as I could tell. I bit one and was surprised to find how tough it was to break with my teeth. It had a distinctly green flavor to it. Glanville then led me back to the lab to begin my education.

Throughout my decade and a half of espresso making, I've used a variety of inexpensive machines, ranging from a $15 Italian stovetop maker to a $200 machine from Starbucks. A couple of years ago, I bought a Rancilio Silvia espresso maker for $500 after reading high praise for it on coffeegeek.com, a Web site with discussion forums, guides, and product reviews about coffee and coffee making. The Silvia is a boxy, no-frills, fully manual espresso maker that looks like it belongs in the galley of a Soviet destroyer. I also bought an $80 burr grinder. Burr grinders produce a much more consistent grind than common cheap blade types, which lacerate beans into shreds of many different sizes. Glanville looked at my grinder approvingly and told me that he used the same model at home. He seemed to be purposely avoiding comment on my Rancilio.

"What do you think of the Rancilio?" I asked him, pressing the issue.

"It's not very good, really," he replied, almost apologetically.

"Really?" I asked. "What machine would you recommend instead that costs $500?"

"Oh, there's nothing better you could buy for that price."

In fact, Glanville was generally against the idea of home-made espresso. His reasons: The hassle of getting and keeping fresh beans, the overall messiness of the procedure, the high cost of decent equipment, and all the finicky requirements needed to pull a quality shot of espresso made it an unsuitable activity for everyone but the most determined home baristas. He said buying a brew system like a Chemex (a glass carafe popular with coffee geeks) would be easier to master and more fun.

Sensing my reluctance to take his advice, he added, "But there's still a lot you can do to get it to make really good espresso. We'll figure out how to do it today."

We decided that the best way to get started was to have me make a cup of espresso while he watched. I poured some beans into the grinder, made sure the fineness dial was at the usual setting, and twisted the timer. Next I pulled out the bin containing the freshly ground coffee and inserted the black plastic scoop that came with the espresso machine. I deposited two scoops of coffee in the Rancilio's filter basket, then grabbed the tamper and pushed down on the coffee, compressing it.

"I know I'm supposed to use thirty pounds of force," I said, grimacing with effort.

Everything I'd ever read about espresso said that thirty pounds is the magic number for tamping down espresso. One of my friends had even made an espresso tamper with a force gauge on it to show him when he was doing it exactly right.

"It doesn't matter how much force you use," Glanville said. "Twenty pounds, forty pounds, eighty pounds. It doesn't matter."

In the first five minutes of my lesson with America's espresso champion, I had learned that my machine was crap and that tamping force didn't matter. I had no idea what other myths were about to be shattered.

Carrying on, I screwed in the portafilter (the metal part with a handle that holds the ground and tamped coffee), placed a cup under it, and turned on the machine. The pump started up and whined for about ten seconds before anything came out. Finally, jet black drops began dribbling out of the portafilter into the cup. "That one's gonna be overextracted," Glanville said. "It shouldn't come out so slowly." After forty-five seconds, the cup had about an ounce of coffee in it, and Glanville shut the machine off. He held the cup to his nose.

"Smell it." He offered it to me, and I took a whiff. "If your coffee smells like burned wheat, then you know that you're overextracted." He lifted the cup and slurped a mouthful, spraying the aerosolized espresso over his taste buds. "Too bitter."

I tried it and had to agree.

"An espresso becomes overextracted when you have too much contact time between the water and the coffee," he said.

He unscrewed the portafilter and slammed it against the rubberized bar in a knock box (a metal container for holding used coffee grounds), ejecting the puck of spent espresso. He pulled out the filter basket and examined the inside of the portafilter. It was blackened like badly tarnished silver. "Before we make the coffee, we have to take a preliminary step and scrub this little guy out. Coffee oils go rancid when they adhere to the metal and dry like that."

I'd never cleaned the filter before. "Should I clean it every month or so?"

"We do it once an hour." Glanville scrubbed it with a small piece of scouring pad until the black stain was gone.

Setting the portafilter aside, he turned his attention to the grinder. "It's grinding the beans too fine," he said. "That's why it was taking so long to extract."

"Where do you set your grinder at home?" I asked him, since he'd attested to owning the same one.

"Oh, I don't use mine for espresso," he said. "For espresso, I would use one of these in here." He pointed at the massive stainless-steel burr grinders in the lab, which cost more than a thousand dollars each. "Your grinder can't give you the consistency you need for espresso. But we'll do the best we can with it." I knew Glanville wasn't trying to be snooty. He genuinely wanted to help me, but I had a feeling he grouped people who made espresso at home with DIY brain surgeons.

Glanville set the grind dial back two notches for a rougher grind and turned it on. Instead of the expected high-pitched whine, it made more of a crunching sound. When it was finished, he pulled out the bin and shook it gently from side to side. He explained that this was to neutralize the static charge that causes ground coffee to clump together. He poured the coffee directly into the filter rather than scooping it in, as I had. It rose from the lip of the filter in a mound. A good deal of coffee spilled over the sides onto the counter.

"It's important to make sure the coffee is distributed evenly in the filter," he said. "The water will find the path of least resistance through the coffee, and if there are irregularities, it'll create a channel and won't touch the rest of the coffee."

Glanville whacked the portafilter down on the countertop, and the coffee settled, becoming nearly level with the rim of the filter.

He then swept his finger along the rim in a practiced circular pattern. The surface was now slightly concave. He pushed down with the tamper once, wiped away some stray particles, tamped again. He then turned the portafilter upside down to let any loose particles fall out. "I do that so they don't get sucked into the machine when you turn off the pump," he said.

"Now, the problem with these inexpensive machines is temperature control. The machines we use have proportional-integral-derivative control, or PID, which keeps the temperature variation to within a couple of tenths of a degree. And it turns out that the temperature of the water is one of the biggest factors in the quality of espresso."

What makes PID so much better than the standard bimetallic thermostat switch found in nearly all lower-end espresso makers? Here's a common analogy: A bimetallic thermostat is like a car that goes at full speed until it reaches a stop sign. At that instant, the driver slams on the brakes. Of course, the car skids right through the intersection, overshooting its mark. Then the driver puts the car in reverse and backs up at full speed, hitting the brakes when it reaches the stop sign, overshooting in the other direction. Back and forth it goes, never stopping at the stop sign itself.

A PID controller is like a car with a driver who sees the stop sign off in the distance and starts applying the brakes lightly. The closer the car gets to the stop sign, the harder the driver applies the brakes. When it reaches the sign, the car is at a dead stop. Like a smart driver, a PID temperature controller heats water to a specified set point and locks it in.

"Since you don't have PID," Glanville continued, "we're gonna do a trick called 'temperature surfing' to keep the water temperature consistent. Before we insert the portafilter with the coffee, we're going to run a certain amount of water through the group head [that part of an espresso machine that squirts out the hot water]. If the water coming out is hissing, we know it's coming out at 212 degrees. With the boiling water as our point of reference, we can actually run water through, and once it stops boiling, we can start to count—'One one-thousand, two one-thousand, three one-thousand, four one-thousand'—and that way we'll have a point of reference and we'll have brought the temperature down to usually around 200 degrees, which is much more optimal for brewing espresso."

Before screwing the portafilter onto my machine, Glanville turned on the pump switch. The water hissed as it poured from the group head. "That's the sign that it's at a boil." After a second or two, the rumbling ceased but water continued to pour out, and Glanville began counting. At "four one-thousand," he snapped the pump switch off, screwed on the portafilter, flipped the switch back on, and set a cup on the tray, all in one fluid motion. Twin spouts of rich-looking caramel-colored, syrupy espresso poured into the cup.

"That's about the proper volume of extraction," he noted. "It looks a little light, so the temperature might have been slightly under. If your coffee looks yellowish, that means your temperature is too low. If it looks really dark, it means your temperature's too high."

"So maybe the surfing should be a little bit less next time?" I asked.

"Exactly. So maybe a three count instead of a four count."

Glanville suggested we try it again with a three count. This time, he used what's called a "naked" portafilter (also known as a "bottomless" or "crotchless" portafilter). It didn't have the two spigots through which the coffee is normally channeled. With a naked portafilter you can see the espresso as it emerges directly from the filter basket, making it easy to detect a faulty tamping job.

Glanville also used a small glass tumbler instead of a cup, so we could see the color of the coffee.

This time he decreed that the coffee was a step closer to perfection, but he wanted to tweak the grind setting again. He made it a bit finer, then turned on the grinder. He unscrewed the portafilter, knocked out the old puck, wiped the filter basket with his apron, filled it with fresh coffee, and made another shot. This time, he said, it was perfect, or at least as close to perfect as one could get using my machine.

"Of course," he said, "if you had PID, you wouldn't have to worry about temperature surfing."

I packed up my stuff and thanked Glanville for the lesson. As I drove home, I thought about his take on amateur espresso making. He didn't think that nonprofessionals could make great espresso, especially without professional-grade equipment. I tried to see it from his perspective. He was, after all, the best espresso maker in the country, with a trophy to prove it. He was comparing his expertise to that of rank amateurs like myself. It had been nice of him to humor me in my fool's errand to make killer espresso. But in the end, I wasn't discouraged. I wanted to make espresso for my friends and myself. The only barista I would be competing against was myself. Still, Glanville had given me plenty of great advice, and I was excited to apply it.

With his temperature-control advice in mind, I went online to look for espresso machines that came with PID. The few that I found were way out of my budget, like the La Marzocco GB/5 Series Group 4 Automatic Volumetric Dosing Espresso Machine, offered for the sale price of $12,879.99 (reduced from $19,870) or even the Vibiemme Double Domobar for $2,000.

I didn't want to give up completely on the idea of PID, because temperature surfing didn't appeal to me, so I looked into the possibility of retrofitting my espresso maker with a PID system. My

Web research revealed that my own Rancilio Silvia happened to be the platform of choice for adding a PID system.

There are a lot of reasons to love the Rancilio. It's got a powerful pump to push water through densely packed, finely ground coffee. It's made of chromed steel, and the boiler and portafilter are made of heavy marine-grade brass. And, for espresso hackers, the Silvia stands above other machines because it's easy to modify. In many ways, it's like a pre-1960 automobile. The electronics are simple, with no microchips, digital readouts, or transistors. The steel cover can be removed with an ordinary Phillips-head screwdriver. And once you take the cover off, you see that there's plenty of room in there. It's easy to access all the inner workings of the machine. You can get your hands inside to add and remove components.

The Silvia is what Mister Jalopy would call "maker friendly," his term for products that can be maintained, repaired, and modified by the owner. He came up with the term (a twist on *user friendly*) after a frustrating experience with his 2000 Chevy pickup. The gas gauge had stopped working. When he took it to the dealer, he was told that the component in the gas tank that sends the fuel-level information to the gauge was faulty and would cost $800 to replace. Mister Jalopy asked the dealer how much it would cost to buy the part so he could install it himself: $500. Why so expensive? he asked. Well, explained the dealer, the fuel sender was connected to the fuel pump, and you had to buy them together as a single part.

That didn't make any sense to Mister Jalopy. The truck's fuel pump was fine. Why buy a new one just to get a fuel sender? He didn't believe that the dealer knew what he was talking about, so he shopped around at a number of auto-parts stores, only to discover that the dealer was right. You had to buy an assembly with both the sender and the pump. He ended up getting one at a discount-parts store for $259. After installing the new assembly (which involved draining and removing the gas tank), he performed an autopsy on the old one.

The fuel sender was connected to the pump by two plastic tabs and a wire connector. He effortlessly removed the fuel sender from the pump with a pair of pliers. Inspecting it, he immediately spotted the problem: A metal tab that connected to a resistor had snapped off. This five-cent part was the root of the problem, but he had just spent $259 to fix it.

Now, Mister Jalopy wasn't upset that the part had stopped working. That would be silly; a car contains thousands of components that are subjected to all kinds of electrical, chemical, and mechanical stresses. What isn't acceptable is designing a part that can't be fixed or replaced by the car's owner.

Mister Jalopy's experience led him to dream of a world of manufactured goods that were open to tinkering by the end user. He sat down and wrote a list of qualities a product should possess in order to be considered "maker friendly." This Maker Bill of Rights was as follows:

▶ Meaningful and specific parts lists shall be included.
▶ Cases shall be easy to open.
▶ Batteries shall be replaceable.
▶ Special tools are allowed only for darn good reasons.
▶ Profiting by selling expensive special tools is wrong, and not making special tools available is even worse.
▶ Torx [a type of screw head] is OK; tamperproof [screw head] is rarely OK.
▶ Components, not just entire subassemblies, shall be replaceable.
▶ Consumables, like fuses and filters, shall be easy to access.

▶ Circuit boards shall be commented [i.e., the components shall be labeled].

▶ Power from USB is good; power from proprietary power adapters is bad.

▶ Standard connectors shall have pinouts defined [i.e., documentation explaining what each wire in the connector does].

▶ If it snaps shut, it shall snap open.

▶ Screws are better than glues.

▶ Documents and drivers shall have permalinks and shall reside for all perpetuity at archive.org [a massive historical backup of the Web].

▶ Ease of repair shall be a design ideal, not an afterthought.

▶ Metric or standard, not both.

▶ Schematics shall be included.

Most companies aren't interested in creating maker-friendly products, but sometimes, apparently by accident, a product comes off the assembly line that way. The Rancilio Silvia is just such a machine. It was introduced in 1997, not as a commercial product but as a thank-you gift to importers and vendors of Rancilio's expensive restaurant-grade espresso machines. Unsurprising, then, that the machine shares many characteristics of commercial equipment—robustness and repairability being chief among them.

When Rancilio decided to offer the Silvia for home use, the coffee hacking community quickly adopted it as a hackable platform for all kinds of experimental modifications. The folks on alt.coffee, the early hangout for espresso geeks, ran Silvia through her paces, carefully recording and reporting the data they collected. The Silvia became the most well-documented espresso maker in history thanks to its legion of hacker fans, who studied every detail of its inner workings and shared them on the Internet. They also obtained the Silvia's schematics from Rancilio and made them available as PDF files. They began calling the machine "Miss Silvia," which shows the level of affection its owners had for it. People merely get by with their affectless Mr. Coffee, but for these coffee hackers there's a real personal relationship with Miss Silvia.

Coffee geeks concluded that Silvia was a fine machine but that her main shortcoming was, as Glanville told me, poor temperature control. Like most consumer-grade machines, it uses a bimetallic thermostat. When the water is cold, the electric current travels through the thermostat to the heating element, which heats up the water. When the water gets hot enough, the thermostat clicks off. (It does this because it's made of a strip of two layers of different metals with different rates of thermal expansion, which causes it to curve in one direction or the other, either making or breaking contact with the electrical circuit that powers the boiler.) The problem with this type of thermostat is that when it clicks off and cuts power to the heater, the heater is still very hot and will continue to heat the water. Then, when the temperature drops enough for the thermostat to click back on, the temperature will keep dropping until the heater gets hot again.

The experimenters on alt.coffee who took temperature measurements of the Silvia discovered that when the heating-element light is off (which means it's ready to pull a shot of espresso), the temperature can vary by as much as 40 degrees.

This amount of variation makes consistently good espresso a nearly impossible dream. But because the Silvia had so many other good qualities (including ease of tinkering), the alt.coffee gang decided not to abandon the machine. Instead, they compensated for the shortcoming by developing the "temperature surfing" technique Glanville had taught me. In early February 2001, an alt.coffee regular named Greg Scace performed a temperature analysis of the Silvia. He measured the temperature of the water as it exited the group head into the portafilter using a somewhat complicated temperature surfing method invented by Mark Prince (a.k.a. "Coffeekid") called "cheating" (others call it "tickling") Miss Silvia. Scace concluded that Coffeekid's technique "worked like a charm," with a temperature variation of just 1 degree, a forty-fold improvement.

In that same month, another alt.coffee member, Andy Schecter, posted that he had replaced the Silvia's stock bimetallic thermostat with a PID temperature controller. (He was familiar with them from his work at National Institute of Standards and Technology.) After programming (or tuning) the PID, he discovered that it kept the water temperature in the boiler from varying by more than a degree or two.

To the rapt readership on alt.coffee, Schecter wrote, "In my mind this is a TREMENDOUS improvement in the Silvia's espresso-making ability."

A month later Greg Scace became the second person to install a temperature controller in his Silvia. He was delighted with the results. He wrote, "I'm really getting off on having implemented PI control. It drove me nuts to have to toggle the hot water switch to tickle Silvia into turning on the heater, then waiting 35 seconds to pull a shot. Now I just look at the temperature readout, smile like a demented caffeine-addled malcontent, and hit the switch at my pleasure. My coffee is as good as when I was tickling Miss Silvia."

That same day, Chris Beck reported that he'd successfully added PID control to his Silvia after consulting with Schecter about how to do it. That made three PID modders. After that, the hack moved like wildfire through alt.coffee. Soon, a number of enterprising coffee hackers were selling kits that included everything you needed to add a PID controller to your espresso machine.

I asked Glanville to recommend a PID kit for my Silvia, and he told me about an add-on kit that didn't require any drilling, cutting, or soldering. It was made by a fellow named Jim Gallt from Lexington, Kentucky. I went to his site, pidkits.com, and ordered it. It cost $280 (about half what I paid for the Silvia itself). A few days later, a shoebox-sized package arrived. Inside, I found several plastic bags containing electronic components, wiring, installation hardware, and a CD. I popped the CD into my computer and read through the instructions.

As I mentioned earlier, Silvia owners like to refer to Silvia as a girl, and the instructions that came with Gallt's kit were no different. ("Lay Silvia down on her back, so that the front switches and logo are pointing straight up.") Like many other kits sold by individuals, the instructions were clear and accessible, a far (and welcome) cry from the awful assembly instructions that come with products imported from China. Gallt's PID kit was lovingly made. All the cables were in a Ziploc bag, looped neatly, with the terminals prefastened to the ends. He even included a tiny tube of thermally conductive paste to apply to the thermostat, stating it was "optional."

Installing the PID controller in my Silvia was a lot of fun. After removing the cover from the machine to expose its innards, I attached a relay to an inner wall with a bolt and nut. Relays are very common in electrical circuits. Unlike a mechanical switch—such as an ordinary light switch, which requires a finger to physically flip it on or off—a relay uses electricity to turn a switch on or off. (The giant computers developed over the course of World War II used thousands of electromechanical relays to perform their calculations, and the resulting clicks reportedly sounded like a cascade of Ping-Pong balls dropping onto a hard floor.) The relay in the temperature-control system waits for a low-voltage signal to be sent from the PID controller to turn the boiler on or off.

The next step was to remove the wiring from the existing

boiler thermostat and replace it with a thermocouple, which is used by the PID controller to measure the temperature of the boiler. The PID controller is basically a tiny computer with a program that measures the current temperature, calculates the difference between the current temperature and the target temperature, and measures how quickly the temperature is changing. With this information, the program figures out how to get to the set point as quickly as possible without overshooting in either direction. It sends a series of "on" or "off" voltage pulses to the relay, which then turns the boiler on or off.

When the temperature is very close to the set point, the relay will turn the boiler on for a fraction of a second at a time, making the indicator lamp blink like a Christmas tree light. The PID controller also has an LED display with two lines of information: the current temperature and the target temperature. Most alt.coffee folks say that 228 degrees (measured on the outside of the boiler; the water temperature is lower) is the sweet spot for espresso. A couple of small buttons on the PID let you adjust the set-point temperature if you feel like experimenting.

It took me about four hours total to install the PID controller system. As I later discovered, making something from a kit is a very different experience from making a chicken coop or a cigar-box guitar from scratch, a process full of trials and errors, misdrilled holes, split wood, crooked angles, nips, tucks, and last-ditch workarounds. Still, I learned a lot about how the espresso machine worked, and following the how-to instructions still gave me the opportunity to use my hands and get lost in the flow of *making*.

Finished with the install, I put the covers back on, carried the machine into my kitchen, filled the tank with water, and turned it on. The temperature started out around 70 degrees and began to rise, silently and steadily. As it got close to 228, the boiler light began flashing, indicating that the relay was turning the boiler on and off. Unlike the electromechanical relays in old computers, this relay had no moving parts and was perfectly silent. In a few minutes the temperature hit 228. It overshot to 228.2 and then backed down to 228, never varying by more than 0.2 degree.

I ground up some Black Cat beans, tamped them down in the portafilter, and pulled my first PID-enhanced shot. Twin rivulets of caramel espresso poured into the cup, topped with a thick layer of *crema*. It tasted as good as the best espresso I'd ever made. Never again would I have to deal with the hassle of temperature surfing. This one variable had been locked down for good. I lifted my demitasse cup in celebration of this small triumph. I had opened a machine, modified it, and made it mine. It felt terrific.

Not everyone thinks PID is terrific. Temperature-surfing diehards say PID takes away from the art and joy of making espresso. They would *really* hate the machine we use in the offices of *Make* magazine. You dump whole beans into one bin and water into another, stick a cup under the nozzle, and press a button. The machine grinds the beans, loads the portafilter, tamps it down, dispenses the shot, and ejects the puck of used coffee grounds into a waste bin. It's clean, quick, and very tasty.

The question is, when you have a machine that does everything for you, do you care less about the coffee? If all the skills that go into making espresso can be perfected with technology, what's left for the home barista to do besides drink? In espresso circles, as in other areas of the DIY movement, there are two camps. One believes that the more involved you are in the process of making something, the better the experience. Making espresso with a fully manual machine is a skill that rewards practice and invites experimentation. Others believe that DIY is a means to an end, and that designing a machine to do something faster, more predictably, and more precisely than you could on your own is the reward. I see both sides. In my experience, DIY is rewarding because you are involving yourself in creative processes, which could include making espresso manually or making the automated system that makes the coffee. The purpose of DIY is learning to take back control of your life from outside parties, and either path can lead you toward independence.

The most rewarding activities are those that offer new challenges over time, and making espresso is one of these. Shortly after adding the PID to my machine, I made a "naked" portafilter by grinding off the nozzles with a carbide cutting bit. Now the espresso pours directly out of the filter into the cup. You can learn a lot about coffee by watching it come out of the filter. If the stream has vertical lines of dark and light *crema* in it (known as "tiger striping"), then it's a good sign that the espresso is going to be excellent. Once the tiger striping diminishes and the stream starts "blonding," you should shut the pump off, because the blond portion is weak and doesn't add anything good to the espresso. If the coffee gushes out in one or more spots on the filter, it means that you've done a poor job of tamping the grounds and that the water is racing through channels without properly extracting the coffee. With my naked portafilter I've gotten to be pretty good at reading streams. My future espresso plans include buying green coffee beans (which are less expensive and keep longer than roasted beans) and roasting them myself in a small-batch roaster I'll make and set up in the backyard.

I've had my Silvia with PID for over a year now and have pulled at least a thousand shots on it. I can't claim that I've pulled a large number of Godshots, but as often as not, the espresso tastes as good as any I've had at Peet's or at independent espresso houses. (It's always better than Starbucks, which has become the espresso of last resort for me, either because my taste buds have grown accustomed to better coffee or because Starbucks isn't as good as it used to be.)

Every time I use my Silvia (about three times a day when I'm not traveling), I'm reminded of how I customized the machine to make it work the way I wanted it to and how, in the process, I gained an understanding of how it actually works. As my friend Charles Platt wrote in his excellent guide, *Make: Electronics*, "By learning how technology works, you become better able to control your world instead of being controlled by it. When you run into problems, you can solve them instead of feeling frustrated by them."

Besides the knowledge about technology I'd picked up, I had also become more aware of the process of making the espresso, and I now pay more attention to the flavor. My friends have benefited from all of this, too. We had about thirty of them at our house the next Thanksgiving, and I was pulling shots for everyone all night long, getting lots of compliments on the quality of the espresso along the way. I was in my glory.

# 5 RAISING BABY DINOSAURS

**"Regard it as just as desirable to build a chicken house as to build a cathedral."**
—FRANK LLOYD WRIGHT

Imagine owning a little robot that could patrol the yard around your house—killing poisonous bugs, fertilizing the lawn, providing entertainment, and magically converting waste products into healthy food. How much would you pay for such a robot? Two hundred dollars? Two thousand? If you buy a chicken, which does all this and more, you'll only have to pay two.

When I was three years old, my grandparents ran a motel in Denver. They also raised turkeys, which roamed freely about the property, mingling with the guests. They were giant animals, weighing as much as I did and standing nearly as tall.

One summer afternoon, some guests were sitting in metal lawn chairs in the backyard, chatting with my grandparents. A half-dozen turkeys, fearless of humans, scratched for bugs in the grass nearby. One of the guests was a large man who wasn't wearing a shirt. His skin was very pale, and he had a few big, dark moles on his flank. One of the turkeys approached him and froze a couple of feet away, studying him carefully. The man, busy talking, didn't pay any attention, but I knew the turkey was up to something.

Slowly it tiptoed closer and closer. When it was about a foot away, it shot its long neck forward and bit off one of the man's large moles. The turkey ran away with the mole gripped in its beak. I was hypnotized by the blood gushing from the wound.

After that, I avoided the turkeys as much as possible, fearful they'd do the same thing to me if they got the chance. Once in a while, a tom would charge and chase me across the yard, which made me like the birds even less.

My grandparents also kept chickens, and I liked them much more. For one thing, they were a lot smaller and less intimidating. For another, they were curious and clever, and their reptilian manner and sharp eyes gave them a trace of ancient mysteriousness. I liked the odd sounds they made and the way they operated as a seemingly telepathic team.

Twenty-four billion chickens are alive today, making them the most successful birds on the planet. Their popularity is due to the fact that they're a cheap source of nutrition for people. Being social creatures, chickens flock together, don't like to wander far from home, and are easy to pen. They can get by on little more than bugs, seeds, lizards, weeds, and table scraps. They're prolific egg layers, and they grow quickly. A broiler chick goes from the roost to the roaster in just six weeks.

Chickens were of great interest to Charles Darwin. In 1868 he catalogued every breed he could find and discovered that they all originated from the wild jungle fowl of southern Asia, which looks like a smaller, more colorful version of the brown leghorn. People began domesticating the birds around five thousand years ago by providing them with food scraps and a place to roost. Over time, selective breeding led to species that could lay large eggs on an almost daily basis.

# BUILDING A COOP

A few years ago Mister Jalopy gave me a book he'd picked up at a garage sale, called *Living with Chickens*. He gave it to me because I had told him that I planned to turn the dilapidated shack behind our house into a chicken coop. Unfortunately, every time I went out back to look at the shack, I lost all motivation to do so. It was full of cans of paint, expired swimming pool chemicals, rusty metal shelving, and filthy layers of dried leaves. The sight of the mess would send me straight back to my home office to browse the Web, a place where "cleaning up" means dragging files into a cartoon trash can.

I finally got the push I needed when I met one of our neighbors at a block party. At the time, we were living in a rural pocket of Tarzana called Melody Acres, which was zoned for farm animals and horses. The neighbor invited my family to see her chickens. Her Plymouth Barred Rocks were attractive birds, with black-and-white-striped feathers. Sarina, who was ten at the time, got cuddly with the rooster, which reminded me of the way she had held a neighbor's chickens in Rarotonga a few years earlier.

When our neighbor started pulling fat pink-brown eggs from the nesting boxes, that clinched it. I swore to myself that I'd fix the shack into a proper chicken coop.

The next day I put on my rattiest clothes and began pulling the crap out. It was hard to believe how much stuff had been in there. I carted it all to a far corner of the yard, and the resulting pile looked like three sheds' worth of junk.

Once I got everything out, I gave the shack a thorough hosing-down, inside and out. The concrete floor tilted slightly, and because there was no drain, the water pooled. It took about twenty minutes with a push broom to get the water out the door. The dirt in front turned to mud, which gave me the excuse I needed to stop for the day.

The next afternoon, I removed a broken wooden gate attached to the left side of the shack, as it served no purpose other than to scrape me with the rusty nail poking out of it whenever I walked by. I put the lumber in the junk pile destined for the dump. I also had to deal with the fence that separated my property from my neighbor Richard's. Originally attached to the side wall of the shack, it had become separated from it over time and was now leaning into Richard's yard, close to falling over. I tried pulling the fence upright so I could resecure it, but it wouldn't budge. I discovered that it was being pushed away by a fast-growing woody vine ten feet away from the shack.

I started lopping away at the vine with a chainsaw and garden shears. The lawn had been watered earlier in the day, so I quickly became covered in mud. Sharp branches poked me at every opportunity. The coop, the fence, and the vines were conspiring against me. It was a classic case of resistentialism, a word coined by Paul Jennings in a 1949 essay for *The Spectator* about his theory that things have a secret agenda to make us miserable by fighting back against our efforts to use them. Resistentialism, he wrote, is encapsulated in the old French saying *"Les choses sont contre nous"* ("Things are against us").

While Jennings's essay is a humor piece, there's some truth in it. Inanimate objects don't have intentions, of course, but people often react as though they do. Have you ever cursed at a snagged garden hose or smacked a cabinet door that pinched you? If you have, you are a resistentialist. I wonder how many people have sworn off DIY because they have the feeling that things are against them.

Carla came out to see where I'd disappeared to, and when she saw me, she asked me what I was doing. I explained that I was fixing the coop.

"But the coop is over there," she said, pointing to where it stood, ten feet away.

"Things are against me," I explained.

She went back in the house.

--- --- --- --- ---

Several hours later, I was sweaty, mud-caked, and tired, but I had finished clearing the vines away from the shack, and the fence was free to move. Richard kindly offered to push against the fence from his side while I fastened it to the shack's sturdy vertical posts.

With these preliminary matters out of the way, I had a blank slate to work with. I inspected the shack and made a to-do list:

1. Build a new door to replace the rotten one.
2. Remove the worn-out roof shingles and replace them with a galvanized-tin roof.
3. Tear the rusty chicken wire from the vertical posts.
4. Add wood siding to the lower part of the shack so dead leaves and dirt won't blow in.
5. Add new chicken wire to the upper part.
6. Paint.
7. Build nesting boxes.
8. Add trim wood and do final touch-up painting.
9. Buy hay, chicken feed, troughs, water trays, etc.
10. Buy chickens.

The door was disintegrating. Pieces of wood at the bottom were crumbling apart, making the door wobble when I opened or closed it. Not only that, but the design looked ugly to me. Why had it been braced with pieces of wood forming an **H** inside the frame? It didn't appear especially sound. I was eager to get rid of it and make a new one from scratch.

I took the old door off, laid it on the ground, and measured its dimensions. Then I went to Home Depot to buy some lumber and wood fasteners. Wandering down the lumber aisle with my shopping cart, I came across some appropriately sized pieces called "furring strips." I didn't know what a furring strip was, but it looked like a good choice for a lightweight chicken coop door, so I bought enough to make the frame plus an extra 50 percent to allow for screwups.

I also bought a rectangle of plywood, screws, and some metal L and T brackets.

I used a clamping miter box to cut the 45-degree angles for the frame and used the brackets to join the pieces. Things were going surprisingly well until I tried to attach the fourth piece and discovered that the furring strips I bought were so twisted that I couldn't complete the frame without seriously warping it. The wood was against me.

Fortunately, I had that extra piece of furring strip, and it seemed straight, so I cut it to size. But again, the frame wouldn't fit together! Each piece was apparently twisted just a little, and when I put the four together, the twistiness was multiplied fourfold. I didn't want to make another trip to Home Depot unless I absolutely had to, so I forged ahead with the less-than-perfect materials at hand, forcing the pieces into position.

I screwed the old hinges onto the finished door and attached it to the shack. The door was still warped, but it turned out that the warping worked in my favor, giving the door a springiness that kept it tight against the jamb when it was latched shut. I felt as though I had tricked the warped wood into submission. Its orneriness had backfired on it. Take that, wood!

All said and done, it had taken a couple of days to build and install the door. Next, I went to work on the roof. When I was in the third grade, my classroom was a corrugated-metal Quonset hut on the agricultural plains of Colorado, and ever since then I'd longed for a building of my own with a corrugated-tin roof. The chicken coop would be my chance to realize that dream. Home Depot had what I needed: roof panels and a tin piece that fit along the peak. (I also bought a roll of screened wire to replace the rusty chicken wire I'd ripped out.)

While I was on the roof tearing off the old tiles (more junk for the junk pile), Richard came over to chat. He told me that the people who used to live in my house had used the shack as a rabbit hutch. One by one, the baby rabbits would escape and dig under the fence into his yard, where they'd fall in the pool and drown. He'd find them in the filter basket.

I assured Richard that my chicken coop was going to be the Fort Knox of poultry enclosures.

The grimy business of removing the disintegrated shingles was delayed by a piece of wood screwed into the roof at a crazy angle. I'm guessing that the rabbit tycoon used it to patch up the plywood under the shingles; eventually the plywood became so rotten it split.

I thought about removing the entire panel of plywood and replacing it. I decided against it, though, because it measured about six by seven feet and was very heavy. Instead, I used my jigsaw to cut off the rotten part, then replaced it with a couple of fence slats from the gate I'd torn down a day or two earlier. This marked the first of many trips to my junk pile to scavenge for materials. I eventually came to the realization that my projects tended to supply themselves as I tore down the old to build the new.

I was having an easy time screwing the lightweight galvanized-tin panels into the roof. I didn't even have to use tin snips, because three panels made a perfect fit on each side of the roof—at least they did on the front side. I hit a snag on the back: After I'd screwed down two panels, I laid down the third and was surprised to see that a wedge-shaped area of the roof plywood was exposed. Had I placed the other panels down at an angle so that they weren't square with the roof? I checked carefully and decided that I had indeed messed up. I unscrewed the panels and started again, trying as much as possible to keep everything square. But the third panel still didn't cover the roof. I had to conclude that the roof wasn't built square.

In his book *A Place of My Own: The Education of an Amateur Builder,* Michael Pollan writes about the nearly disastrous repercussions of accidentally skewing a corner away from a perfect right angle in the frame of a small office-house he was building in the woods near his house. Because of that one mistake, he had to make custom angle cuts for every window and door frame, for the floor, for the roof, and for almost everything else. It was a nightmare. He finished the house, but it took much longer than it would have if everything had been square to begin with.

Now I faced the same problem. I saw three options: (1) I could try to rebuild the roof to make it square, (2) I could buy an extra tin panel and trim a wedge-shaped section to cover the exposed area, or (3) I could cut the overhanging portion of the plywood to match the edge of the tin roof panel. I went with option 3. I figured, if it looked terrible, I would go ahead and rebuild the roof to make it square.

I got on a ladder and used a jigsaw to cut a wedge of plywood from the roof. The overhanging wood almost touched the roof beam at the lower end of the roof slope. My hopes weren't high that this would work out, but I went ahead and screwed the final roof panel onto the plywood. What do you know—it went from ugly to barely passable. I asked Carla to come out and take a look. I didn't tell her about the problem, because I wanted to see if she would notice it on her own. She's pretty observant.

"It looks great."

At this stage, my chicken coop had been cleaned out, given a new door, and topped with a tin roof. The next step was to add a fourth wall. The previous owner had run chicken wire from floor to ceiling on one side instead of building a wall. This allowed dust and leaves to blow in. I don't understand why he did it that way. His rabbits must have been dirty and miserable. I wanted clean, happy chickens.

My first thought was to go to Home Depot and pick up some plywood, but, as Mister Jalopy once told me, as soon as you cross your property line, you might as well write off the possibility of getting anything else done that day. Remembering this sage advice, I opted to use whatever scraps I had lying around the yard. I found a nice, solid piece of plywood left over from a remodeling job done on our house the previous summer. That took care of the first vertical foot or so. What would I use for the next couple of feet?

I suddenly thought of the fence slats from the gate. The wood was weathered and gray, but it was rot-free and straight. I used a trash can as a workbench, pulled out the jigsaw, and cut the slats to length. To fasten the plywood and slats to the shack's framing, I used coated drywall screws, which are guaranteed not to rust. (I prefer screws to nails because I don't like the loud noise a hammer makes, and it seems to me that wood always works its way loose from nails.)

With the siding out of the way, it was time to paint the shed. The previous homeowners had left a five-gallon bucket of brilliant white semigloss interior/exterior paint, and it was about two-thirds full. It seemed a little thicker than it should be, probably because it was getting on in years and had started to coagulate, but I diluted it with water. Jane, who had become intensely curious about the chicken coop, insisted on helping me paint as soon as she saw me with the brush and bucket. I put her to work on the back. She got about half the paint on the coop; the rest went on her hair and clothes. She got bored after painting a small scrawly patch. I had to wipe her down before she went back in the house.

As I painted the beams and the siding, it became clear to me that a lot of the original lumber that was on the shack, especially the plywood, was rotten, and that no amount of paint was going to make it better. I had to replace those spots with solid wood. This ended up being one of the most time-consuming parts of the job.

It took almost the entire summer to finish the coop. I didn't work on it every day, but I spent at least a couple of hours a few times a week on it—finishing the paint job, adding the wire screen, building the enclosure where the chickens would sleep, and making the little inclined ramp they would use to climb into the enclosure to sleep. But far from finding it drudgery, I enjoyed the time I spent working on the coop. I often got lost in a museum of memories. There was no telling where my mind would wander—an afternoon as an eight-year-old stringing up a wire-and-tin-can telephone between my bedroom window and the kid's next door; seeing one of the guys in my college dorm sitting cross-legged on the concrete plaza by himself in the middle of a rainstorm; standing on a deserted street in Japan more than twenty years ago and having my arm pinched by a very old homeless couple who were fascinated by the way Carla and I looked. Memories that I'd long forgotten were somehow dredged up by the activity of making the coop. I never tried to direct my thoughts; I just let them parade through my mind. One of my favorite cartoonists, Seth (he goes by his first name only), wrote an essay for the Canadian magazine *The Walrus* about his similar experience when he draws cartoons:

> When I'm breaking down a strip or hammering out dialogue, I'm using that writer's focus. But drawing and inking are different. They use different parts of the brain. I often find that when I'm drawing,

*only half my mind is on the work—watching proportions, balancing compositions, eliminating unnecessary details.*

*The other half is free to wander. Usually, it's off in a reverie, visiting the past, picking over old hurts, or recalling that sense of being somewhere specific—at a lake during childhood, or in a nightclub years ago. These reveries are extremely important to the work, and they often find their way into whatever strip I'm working on at the time. Sometimes I wander off so far I surprise myself and laugh out loud. Once or twice, I've become so sad that I actually broke down and cried right there at the drawing table. So I tell those young artists that if they want to be cartoonists, the most important relationship they are going to have in their lives is with themselves.*

I wonder if one of the main reasons people garden, or knit, or retire to their garages and basements to tinker, is because they enjoy this unusual state of consciousness. Some people might be able to achieve it by meditating, but using your hands seems to do the trick, too.

## MAIL-ORDER CHICKS

I finished the coop at the end of August. In September, I got a phone call from a clerk at my local post office. She told me that a box containing live chicks had arrived and was waiting for pickup. I'd ordered them a couple of weeks earlier from MyPetChicken .com, which had sent them by overnight mail from Oregon. At the time I got the call, I was two thousand miles away, giving a talk about blogging and online media at the University of Illinois at Urbana-Champaign, so I immediately called Carla at home and asked her to pick up the box. The kids weren't in school that day, so the three of them went to the post office.

Roughly the size of a shoebox, the package was surprisingly small, considering that it had been home to six birds during their trip from Portland to Los Angeles. The half-dozen Barred Plymouth Rock chicks were peeping loudly inside. When my wife opened the box, the tiny two-day-old chicks were huddled together in a nest of straw. Before I'd left for Illinois, I'd prepared a large cardboard box in the room next to my office with pine shavings, an infrared heat lamp, a watering station, and a chick feeder. Carla and the kids placed the chicks in their new home and called to tell me they looked fine. They were no doubt hungry and thirsty, but they weren't in danger of starving or dying of thirst: Chicks are born with enough nutrients and moisture in their system to keep them going for forty-eight hours without suffering. Carla dipped the beak of each chick into the water to teach it where to get a drink, and within moments they were all happily eating and drinking.

For the next several weeks, I took frequent work breaks, pulling a chair up next to the box to observe the chickens. I built a perch for them out of bamboo screwed to blocks of wood. When I set the perch down in the box, the chicks skittered to the far end of the box, huddling so tightly together they looked like a single ball of feathers. After a few seconds, they started stretching their necks out to get a better look at the invader I'd introduced into their sanctuary. A moment later, as their curiosity overtook their fear, they crept toward the perch. One brave chick, reminding me of the australopithecine in the monolith-encounter scene from *2001: A Space Odyssey*, walked over and pecked it. This emboldened the others, which scuttled over in a pack to investigate. By the end of the day, they were hopping on and off the perch without fear.

At six weeks, my hens still weren't close to being full grown, but the twenty-five pounds of chick starter feed they'd eaten had turned them into healthy teenagers. They were ready to be moved to their coop. First, though, I had to line its concrete floor with litter. I didn't relish the thought of mucking out the chicken coop every couple of weeks—in fact, it was one of the things that had previously discouraged me from getting chickens. I was already the designated crap remover of the family: The task of regularly cleaning our cats' litterboxes and our guinea pig's cage had somehow fallen on my shoulders. Now it looked like I was going to be the one who shoveled piles of chicken poop, too.

When I complained about the prospect to my friend Kelly Coyne (coauthor of *The Urban Homestead* with her partner, Erik Knutzen), she told me I ought to practice the "deep litter system." Kelly and Erik adhere to the appealing urban-homesteading notion that "work makes work" and that the best way to deal with a problem is to set it up so that it takes care of itself. Deep litter is just such an example. The idea is to cover the coop's floor with about twelve inches of bedding material (like wood shavings) and let the chickens scratch their manure deep under the surface; there tiny microbes break it down and convert it into nutritious chemicals and minerals, which the chickens ingest as they peck around for the bugs that are attracted to the droppings. Other than the need to add new bedding material once in a while, this ecosystem is nearly maintenance free. The smell isn't really a problem, because the bedding absorbs moisture from the chicken droppings, so they dry up quickly. After a year, you can shovel it out and use the stuff as garden fertilizer.

Deep litter isn't a new idea. The April 1, 1909, issue of a magazine called *Gleanings in Bee Culture* ran an advertisement that praised the deep-litter system as "a wonderful new discovery that will revolutionize poultry-keeping: A 'system' whereby you need not feed, nor clean out the pens oftener than once a month, and yet the results will be far beyond any other method. *Only one dollar for the great secret.*" It goes on to offer some extracts from the booklet to explain how it works, but not in enough detail, of course, to keep the curious poultry farmer from sending in his dollar for the secret.

On the last day of November I let the chickens out of the coop to run around freely for the first time. I was surprised by how quickly they took to it. As soon as I opened the door they bolted out and started scratching in the grass and dirt, grazing on different tree and bush leaves, weeds, blossoms, and blades of grass. They stretched out in the sun and gave themselves dust baths. How amazing that this behavior was already encoded in them! How do they know which things are good to eat, I wondered? Jane and I set up a couple of chairs in the backyard and watched them for two hours in the afternoon sun. When the sky turned to dusk, the chickens lined up and walked back into the coop and up the inclined ramp into their cozy sleeping compartment.

About a week later, Jane asked if we could dress the chickens in different outfits so we could tell them apart. As much as I wished we could, I knew the chickens wouldn't like it. Instead, I retrieved the brightly colored plastic cable ties I kept in my toolbox. Sarina held the chickens while I banded their legs with the ties, each chicken with a different color. This allowed us to note the personality differences between the birds. For instance, black-banded Ethel and pink-banded Rosie were friendly to people, and bolder than the other birds. They were more apt to wander away from the flock to seek out tasty bugs and leaves. Orange Jordan and blue Darla were the shy ones, running away from us if we came near. Yellow Daisy was the flock's security guard. Whenever a squirrel came close, she'd make a warning cluck, sending the rest of the birds into high alert. At Daisy's signal they'd freeze and stretch their necks to get a good look at the squirrel. When it moved far enough away, they'd go back to their business. (Later, when they got bigger, the chickens would chase the squirrels, sending them running up the nearest tree.)

In his book *Living with Chickens: Everything You Need to Know to Raise Your Own Backyard Flock,* Jay Rossier writes that before he started keeping chickens, he thought of them as "stupid, fearful, and aggressive. They are full of sharp points from their beaks to their toes and move in a distinctly jagged way, jerking their heads more like a reptile than a bird." After spending time with his flock, he changed his tune, describing them as "stately, dignified, and industrious creatures."

I agree wholeheartedly with Rossier's assessment of chickens, but I also happen to find their reptilian behavior very interesting. In 2007 I was delighted to read that scientists who had discovered bits of collagen in a sixty-eight-million-year-old *Tyrannosaurus rex* femur concluded that its protein sequences more closely matched those of a chicken than any other living creature's. The sequence similarity between a chicken and a *T. rex* is 58 percent, meaning it's very likely the forty-foot-long dinosaur evolved into the three-pound critters scratching for rollie pollies in my backyard. In fact chickens still have a gene for growing saber-shaped, reptilian teeth. In 2006 a researcher was studying a mutant chicken embryo and noticed formations on the beak that looked liked alligator teeth. Fortunately for us humans, chicks that form these razor-sharp weapons never make it past the embryo stage; otherwise chickens would be dangerous!

Chickens, true to their *T. rex* lineage, are voracious eaters. Besides weeds, grass, and leaves, they go after bugs with gusto. Before we had chickens, our yard was full of snails. We lived in fear of black widow spiders, which lurked under every piece of outdoor furniture. Once I reached for the valve handle on our gas barbecue and almost touched one. (Spiders apparently like the smell of the odorant added to propane, I was told by our pool serviceman, who said he always finds spiders in the air-intake vents of gas pool heaters.) Subsequent to my brush with venom, I found and killed nine black widows in a single day. When I told Carla, she called an exterminator service and they started spraying around our house once a month.

We canceled the exterminator about a month before we got our chickens, because we didn't want to poison them. Fortunately, they made short work of the black widows and of all the other bugs on our property as well. They were even able to jump several inches into the air to snatch flies. Once we let our chickens loose in the yard, we never saw a single spider, snail, slug, grasshopper, cricket, or beetle again. Not spraying for bugs saved us $50 a month. And the chickens' bug diet provided them with a great source of protein and omega-3 fatty acids, which meant their eggs were good for us, too.

Our lawn started getting much greener. The fertilizer the birds deposit all over the lawn plays a role in that, but I also think they eat grubs that damage the grass. For instance, for years our side lawn was plagued by two big dead spots, which grew larger and larger over time. Nothing I tried—extra watering, aerating, fertilizing, seeding—seemed to help. But once we introduced the chickens, clumps of dark green grass began growing in the spots. Someone told me that our lawn troubles had been caused by the grubs of the fig-eater beetle, which also happen to gorge on the delicious figs growing on our tree. If this is true, and the chickens are responsible for making my lawn greener *and* increasing my fig harvest, then they deserve a medal.

The birds were making our lives better in so many ways that it came as a surprise when they started laying eggs, even though eggs were the main reason we had wanted chickens in the first place. At first, we weren't even very eager to eat them. It didn't help that the first few were either asymmetrical or missing their shells. But even after the eggs started to look normal, it took a while for everyone in the family to feel OK about eating something that came out of our pets' bodies. It felt a bit like drinking milk from your cat.

Carla wouldn't taste the first egg I collected. I did so only because I felt I needed to set an example for the rest of the family; I had no appetite for it. I knew I was being silly. I'd never felt this way about a store-bought egg. But store eggs came in cartons kept on refrigerated supermarket shelves, not directly from the warm, gooey cloaca of a bird. My family consumed animal products that came packaged in containers; we'd never given much thought to the source. (I've come to learn that this is a normal reaction. When my kids bring new friends over and show them the eggs in the nesting box, many of the kids are surprised to be told that they're edible. We give them some to take home, and they often keep them as toys, coloring them and even making little houses for them.)

I cooked the first egg in a little butter. The yolk was bright orange and stood up firmly above the clear white. I took this to be a good thing, certainly better than the flattish pale yellow yolks I was accustomed to eating, but at this point any difference between my hens' and store-bought eggs only served to remind me that I was eating something my pet had excreted. I tried to clear my mind before eating the first forkful, but I couldn't get the image out of my head. I ate the egg anyway. It tasted different from the ones I was used to—more flavorful, and fresher. I was still too freaked out to appreciate it, though.

Eventually I learned to savor the superior qualities of my hens' eggs. My wife and kids came around, too. Now the pleasure center in my brain lights up every time I walk to the coop, look in the nesting box, and see a trio or quartet of Silly Putty–colored eggs waiting for me. It's like an Easter egg hunt every day. They are so beautiful and perfectly formed that they seem to have been made by an artist.

# STARTING OVER

It's hard to be a homesteader if you keep changing homes. I've moved twenty-one times since I was born. When we moved into that restored 1930s farmhouse in Tarzana in 2004, I hoped it would be the last time. It was a perfect home for us, or so we thought. It had about a dozen different kinds of fruit trees and a half acre of flat land that could be used for things like outbuildings, animal pens, greenhouses, gardens, and fish ponds. The house itself was bright, open, and cheerful. I'd already killed the front lawn, and I was getting ready to add some raised-bed planters to grow vegetables there. I'd staked out an area of our side yard for starting a fruit orchard. Our friends liked hanging out in the large room that extended the length of the house. The chicken coop was big, rainproof, and comfortable for my hens, which were producing an average total of four nice eggs every day, and they had the run of the yard. It had turned out to be the perfect place to explore self-sufficiency and DIY living.

But in the spring of 2009 we moved to Studio City, for a few reasons. The elementary school in the district was excellent. The climate was milder than in Tarzana, which is the hottest town in Los Angeles. (Summers in Tarzana are scorchers, with multiday runs of three-digit temperatures.) Finally, our new place was a few houses away from Carla's sister, who had a daughter Jane's age. For all these reasons, it made sense to move.

On the other hand, the new house didn't have a chicken coop; I was going to have to either make or buy a new one. For weeks I vacillated. I was tempted by the colorful and stylishly rounded coops made by Eglu, which look a little like the early candy-colored iMac. But I couldn't bring myself to buy a coop made out of plastic. After Carla's complaints the year before about the "hideous" black plastic garden cart, I had been converted to a plastic hater, and there was no going back.

I looked online at the dozens and dozens of wood chicken coops for sale and became paralyzed by the abundance of choices. I couldn't make up my mind. While each coop was different, they all shared something in common that bothered me: They were unnecessarily complicated. Some were built to look like miniature barns, others like little prairie schoolhouses or cottages. I didn't want superfluous ornamentation or a shape that would make it hard to access the interior. I wanted something dead simple: a box raised off the ground with room inside for a nesting box and a roosting perch, nothing else. I decided I'd have to build such a coop myself.

I started to design one using Google SketchUp, a great free application for designing all kinds of stuff, from birdhouses to barns. But after a while I realized I was probably overthinking it. I drove to the lumber store and took a look at what they had. I found six-foot-tall, five-inch-wide fence slats that would work for the walls. The length of the slats dictated the dimensions of the coop: It would be six feet long and three feet deep. Standing in the lumber aisle, I pulled out my phone and used the calculator function to estimate how many slats I'd need: twenty-one. I came across some two-by-twos that looked strong enough to serve as the four stilts keeping the coop off the ground. I bought seven eight-foot-long sticks of the two-by-twos and an equal number of one-by-twos for framing the coop. I also bought a roll of chicken wire (or "poultry fencing," as the manufacturer called it), a pair of door hinges, and a corded electric drill to drive the screws. It took some effort to fit all this into my Volkswagen Beetle, but by folding down the backseat and leaning the front passenger seat all the way forward, I managed to cram everything in.

I drove to our new house (which we hadn't moved into yet) with the materials I'd purchased and carried them into the backyard. It was a warm, clear spring day—coop-building weather. As I measured, cut, drilled, and assembled the pieces of wood according to the rough plan in my head, I thought about how far I'd come since I started my experiment to do and make more things myself. I felt confident about this project because I'd become more familiar with the way lumber behaves. I understood the functions and limitations of the tools. And, perhaps most important, I was comfortable with the idea that I might screw it up. Who cared if I did? As long as I eventually produced a chicken coop that kept my hens safe and dry, it didn't matter what happened.

The coop was coming along nicely, but I still had the problem of how to deal with all the coyotes in the surrounding hills. (We didn't have coyotes back in Tarzana.) I contemplated building some kind of pen to contain the chickens. The thought depressed me. I didn't think my hens, used to free-range living, would enjoy being fenced in. I surely had the happiest chickens on the planet. They had roamed the half acre of our Tarzana home, scratching in the mulch for bugs, nibbling on grass and weeds and toadstools, and taking long dust baths and naps in the sun. It would be sad to take all that away from them. What was I going to do?

I put the thought aside for the time being. I wasn't able to finish the coop in one afternoon, so the next morning I went back to the new house with Carla. I told her I didn't want to pen in the chickens. She reminded me that she had grown up in the Studio City hills and that she had seen a lot of coyotes there. If I let the chickens run around unprotected, it would be their death sentence. I agreed with her. I would have to create a barrier of some kind to keep the coyotes from my chickens. The Studio City house had no front yard to speak of, and the backyard was a fairly narrow strip of grass. Neither would really do for a pen. I started to wonder whether I should even keep chickens here. The people who moved into our Tarzana house told me that they were looking forward to using the coop there to raise chickens of their own. I wondered if I should just give them mine and be done with it.

As I mulled this possibility, I opened the gate to the swimming pool at the Studio City house to look at the area behind it, where I planned to keep my bees. The ground was sloped, and a lot of poorly maintained pepper trees grew there. But it was peaceful, and it had a nice woodsy feel. As I looked around, I realized that the area was completely enclosed by a six-foot-high chain-link fence. The only way to get in or out was through gates. I could put the coop here and give my chickens the run of this shady, grassy, wild hill. They'd love it.

I found a couple of holes in the fence I'd need to patch, but other than that, it would be very difficult for a coyote or other predator to jump it. And the chickens would be safe inside the coop even if a coyote did manage to get over or under the fence after dark.

## THE AUTOMATIC CHICKEN DOOR

It wasn't hard moving the chickens from our old house to the new one. We waited until they were asleep at night, then Sarina and I lifted them one at a time from the perch and deposited them in the back of our car. They peeped with mild protest but were very calm during the twenty-minute drive. Chickens are good travelers.

The new coop I made was small, basically a place for the chickens to sleep at night and lay eggs during the day. I couldn't in good conscience leave the birds in it all morning while they waited for me to wake up and open the door so they could scratch around the yard. The coop in Tarzana had been large enough to allow them to walk and stretch their legs. The new one would literally keep them cooped up.

For the first couple of days after moving into our new house, I set my alarm for 6:30 a.m. so I could let the chickens out. Even at this early hour, they were already clamoring to begin their day of foraging. I've never liked getting up early, and I couldn't imagine having to wake up at that time every morning. I started leaving the large coop door open at night so they could come and go as they pleased, but the chickens didn't like having the door open in the day, because they wanted privacy when laying their eggs in the nesting box. I started finding eggs hidden in bushes and little hollows against the fences.

Adding a small door with a ramp could easily solve that part of the problem. That way I could keep the large door closed all the time, opening it only when I needed to inspect the interior. The ideal solution would be to make an automatic door that was small enough to give them a feeling of privacy when it was open and would close after they'd settled onto their perch for the evening.

I told Carla about my idea, and she was dubious. "How can you trust it to work?" she said. "You have to have a person open and close the door." I said that when we were home, we'd always check to make sure the automatic door worked, but it would really come in handy when we went out at night and saw a late movie, or when we went away for the weekend. She remained unconvinced.

Googling "automatic chicken door" returned a few different designs and commercial products but fewer than I would have expected, given that millions of people keep chickens. Most were designed to either open in the morning or close at night but not both. I didn't want a single-function door. I wanted something that would allow us to leave for a day or two without having to hire a neighbor to let the chickens out in the morning and close the door at night.

I eventually found a design that seemed to work for me. John Beaty, the director of technology programs at Northeastern University in Boston, had built an ingenious door opener out of a motorized drapery puller, used for opening curtains automatically. Drapery pullers are beloved by home-automation enthusiasts—DIYers who use devices to automatically control lights, adjust the temperature of rooms, trigger video cameras, turn appliances off and on, open garage doors, and so on. The beauty of the drapery puller is that when current is applied to it, it turns its motor in one direction (opening the curtain). When current is applied again, the motor reverses direction. Beaty's design incorporated a door that slid up and down, attached to a cord. The drapery puller was plugged into an ordinary timer switch (the kind people use when they go on vacation to turn a lamp on in the evening so potential thieves think the house is occupied). When the timer turned the power on (once in the morning and again at night), a pulley would draw a cord attached to the chicken door up or down.

I ordered a drapery puller online for about $80. I already had an appliance timer switch, and a contractor had left a large pile of scrap material on the side of our house that I was able to pick through for some of the other stuff I needed. I found a length of metal roof flashing to serve as channels for the door to slide up and down in. Beaty had used a thin sheet of aluminum for his door, but I couldn't find one, and I couldn't find any wood that seemed right for the job.

Then I came across a piece of masonite (sporting a painting I'd started and abandoned) that would fit the bill. I cut it to size and inserted it in the slides. Then I attached the drapery puller above the door, hung a chain over its pulley, and attached one end of the chain to the door and the other end to a piece of metal that weighed about the same as the door. (Balancing the load on either end would keep the motor from having to work so hard.) I plugged the puller into an extension cord to test it out. The motor kicked in and lifted the door right up. It worked! I fine-tuned its operation by adjusting a couple of little dials on the drapery puller that controlled how long the motor turned in each direction.

When I was done building it, I brought Carla out to show her how it worked. I opened the main door so she could see the mechanics of the system. I plugged it into the extension cord, and the motor hummed, lifting the door.

"That's so cute!" she exclaimed. I unplugged the cord and plugged it back in to lower the door. "I didn't think it would be so neat," she added.

I live for moments like these.

But I still wasn't finished. I couldn't have a hundred-foot extension cord going from the house to the coop. It was a safety hazard and an eyesore. It needed a permanent power solution. There was a swimming pool pump about twenty-five feet away from the coop. I could tap into it to power my chicken door. Luckily, my father, an electrical engineer by training, was in town helping us settle into our new house. I happily accepted his offer to help me with this part of the project.

My dad and I went to the hardware store and bought some outdoor electrical wires, an underground conduit, an outdoor outlet box, and some other odds and ends. He knew exactly what to get, having done outdoor wiring before. When I was younger and would go with him to the hardware store, I paid little attention to what he was buying or why. Now I realized that this electrical stuff could come in very handy. So I paid close attention.

Back home, we carried the supplies and tools to the pool pump station. After unraveling the electrical conduit, we discovered it wasn't long enough. I drove back down the hill to a small but well-stocked hardware store to buy a longer piece. When I told the clerk what I needed, he asked me what I was planning to use it for.

When I told him I wanted to power my automatic chicken door, he acted like he didn't believe me. I remembered that I had taken a movie of the chicken door opening and closing with my digital camera. I pulled it out and showed him the clip.

"That is so cool!" he said. He was just as impressed with it as Carla had been. He called over the other two clerks and asked me to show them the video. A woman customer got into the huddle, too.

"Wow! That's really neat," said one. The woman asked where I lived.

"Right up the hill."

"And you actually have chickens now?" She was incredulous.

"Yep, six of them."

"Are you going to eat them?"

"No, they're pets, but we eat their eggs."

"Really? They lay eggs?"

"Sure," I said. I gave her the whole *Omnivore's Dilemma* rap about how the yolks were orange, round, firm, and bouncy, unlike the pale, flat, runny yolks you get with store-bought eggs. The small crowd looked at me with amazement and no small degree of respect in their eyes. I was being recognized for being a DIYer, someone who could get things done. In a society where most people solve problems by buying solutions instead of making them, even inept DIYers like me are regarded with a degree of awe.

Returning home, still basking in the glow of the admiration of strangers, I found my dad at the pool pump, getting started on the wiring. He had unscrewed the electrical power panel and stuck the probes of a voltmeter into a pair of terminals. It read "117 volts AC." He turned off the circuit breaker so he could attach the wires from the electrical cord we'd just purchased. I was glad he was around, because I would have had a very hard time figuring out what to do. When he ran into trouble attaching the wires directly to the terminals, he cut some of the wires that were already attached to the power panel's terminals and used wire nuts (colored plastic things that look like tiny ice cream cones) to splice the wires together.

With one end of the cord taken care of, he wired up the outlet box to the other end and attached it to the interior of the chicken coop. I plugged the appliance timer into the outlet and plugged the drapery puller into the timer. We turned the circuit breaker back on, and I tested the door by turning the wheel of the timer until it clicked at the 6 a.m. mark. *Whirrrr*—the door rose! When it stopped, I turned the wheel until it reached the 9 p.m. mark. *Whirrrr*—the door shut.

I shot another video of the door in action and posted it to my blog. Mister Jalopy e-mailed me right away: "I watched the door open/close video three times! It is mesmerizing! Good job, Mark!"

Who knew that making a chicken door could be so beneficial to one's self-esteem?

## THE COYOTES

The chickens had no problem learning the operation of the door. They walked down the ramp when the door opened, and walked up the ramp when it started to get dark. The door closed at 9 p.m., after they'd been inside for an hour or so. They were laying eggs in the nesting box, which I retrieved through a little access hole in the coop wall.

For a week, this arrangement worked without a hitch. Then, one Saturday morning, our life of chicken bliss was shattered. I awoke to the sound of my chickens squawking. I checked the clock: It was 6:15 a.m. That meant the automatic door was open and the chickens were out. Still sleepy, I didn't think much of their clucks at first. But they kept at it. The sound they were making was unusual. A bad feeling crept over me.

"I'm going to check on the chickens," I told Carla, who was just starting to wake up.

Outside the dawn light was weak. I saw four chickens standing on the sloped part of the property above the coop. They were standing tall, with their necks straight and long, and were clucking loudly. They all stared at the same spot down the hill. I turned to see what they were looking at. A skinny gray coyote was standing on our side of the fence. I felt a gush of panic and yelled, "Get out!" The coyote scrambled up the chain-link fence and disappeared into the scrubby vegetation of the valley below.

My heart pounding, I looked for the missing two chickens, but I already knew I wasn't going to find them, at least not alive. I walked down to where the coyote had been standing. Before I got there, I found clumps of black-and-white-striped feathers in the grass. I was surprised by how many there were. Then I saw a chicken slumped against the fence. She was lying upside down, with her legs exposed. One of them had a green cable tie around it. Hazel had been killed. She was the kids' second-favorite chicken, right behind Ethel. The two of them were the boldest, friendliest, and most inquisitive hens in the flock. I looked around for another chicken body but couldn't find one.

I went in the house to tell Carla the news. She followed me out, and I explained what had happened. She started crying. I looked at the leg bands of the four surviving chickens: Darla, Jordan, Daisy, and Rosie. That meant that Ethel, the black-banded hen, was gone. I looked around, but there was no sign of her, except perhaps the feathers blowing from one clump of weeds to another. The coyote must have carried her over the fence.

Carla was upset not only because the two chickens had been

killed but because she had warned me about the coyotes and had (correctly) believed I hadn't done enough to ensure the chickens' safety. She'd told me that she didn't think the fence was high enough to prevent coyotes from getting over it. I'd been wrong, and now our two favorite chickens were dead.

It had been a bad idea to bring the chickens here, where coyotes were rampant, I decided. "Maybe I can find someone to keep them," I thought. I'd have to make a decision about it, but right now I needed to come up with a way to keep the chickens safe for the rest of the morning, until the coyotes went to sleep. I sat in a lawn chair and played chicken shepherd while Carla went back into the house.

After the sun was fully out and I felt reasonably safe that the coyotes wouldn't be coming back, I took stock of my building supplies. I had some extra chicken wire and some fencing posts, so I spent about an hour making a circular enclosure surrounding the coop. It was only four feet high, and no match for a hungry coyote, but it would keep the chickens contained so I could keep my eye on them. When I completed the makeshift enclosure, I had to gather up the chickens, which wasn't easy, because they were spooked and ran away from me when I got near them. Eventually I managed to collect them all and deposit them inside the wobbly circular boundary. I didn't feel great about leaving the chickens alone, but I went inside and made breakfast for the family, frequently going out to check on the chickens.

After breakfast Carla called a few of her friends and told them what had happened. They were all self-styled coyote experts, offering suggestions about what could be done. One said we needed to line our perimeter with razor wire. Another suggested an electric fence. One friend said we needed to bait the area with poisoned meat.

I went online and looked at the Los Angeles County Web site

about dealing with coyotes. It recommended building six-foot fences with fourteen-inch angled extenders all around. The site also said that the entire fence "should have some sort of galvanized wire apron buried at least 4 to 6 inches in the ground, which extends out from the fence at least 15 to 20 inches. The apron should be securely attached to the bottom of the fence. Coyotes are very adept diggers and prefer to dig under fences rather than jump them."

This seemed like a tremendous amount of hard, expensive work—exactly the kind of DIY project I loathe. What's more, I doubted it would work. With a piece of property as large as the one we were living on, and with a great deal of the perimeter bordering the canyon wilderness, the coyotes would surely figure out a way to breach the barrier. I decided I'd much rather build a coyote-proof pen attached to the coop where the chickens could spend their daylight hours, even if it meant that their free-range days would be over. I knew it would take some planning to make a pen that was both secure and attractive, but first I needed to make some kind of temporary pen better than the flimsy chicken-wire fence I'd slapped together. I drove to Home Depot—I was becoming the cornerstone of their business by this point—and bought eleven metal fence posts, fifty feet of wire screen, and one hundred cable ties.

When I got home, Carla told me that I wouldn't be able to start working on the new enclosure, because we had to get ready for Jane's sixth birthday party and I needed to pick up the cake and other snacks. Besides, the house was still in a state of disarray because of our recent move—every room was filled with unpacked boxes. I'd been out of town for the last few days, so I hadn't been able to help unpack. And the little time that I had been in town had been spent almost exclusively on dealing with the chickens.

"I'm going to write my own book," Carla said. "It'll be about living with a crazy chicken man." She realized that the stuff I was doing was necessary, but she also said that my DIY projects were exacerbating the stress that always comes with moving into a new house.

After the birthday party, my friend Mark, who happens to be a contractor, came over to help me put together a better temporary chicken pen. It was late afternoon, and dusk was approaching. I felt rushed. Doing this project was a lot different from the slow-living projects I'd been working on. This was a matter of chicken life or death. It was DIY as a necessity, not as therapy or a hobby. After pounding in the fence posts and attaching the wire screen to them, Mark and I made a roof beam out of a three-by-three piece of lumber and draped the chicken wire over it. Now the fence would be completely closed in. The automatic chicken door led directly into the pen. I laid a blue plastic tarp over the chicken wire to provide some shade for the chickens. The finished structure wasn't nice to look at, but I hoped it would be good enough to protect the hens in the daytime.

Mark had to leave to pick up a relative at the airport, so I continued to work on the pen myself, figuring I had about an hour and a half to go. I happened to glance down at the area where the coyote had hopped over the fence. On the other side, I saw a mass of black-and-white feathers that I hadn't noticed earlier. I dropped my tools and walked down the slope to see what it was. When I got close enough, I realized that it was a chicken—and it was alive.

Had one of the four survivors managed to escape the new enclosure and somehow get over to the other side of the fence without my knowing it? It was beginning to get dark, and I needed to get the chicken back on our side of the fence before a coyote grabbed it. I climbed over with difficulty and dropped down to the other side. The hen was peeping quietly. I picked her up and looked at her leg band. It was black.

Ethel! She had survived the coyote attack!

I quickly examined her body for injuries, but the tough little bird seemed to be in perfect shape. I called to my brother-in-law, who was in the backyard, and handed him the chicken before climbing over the fence myself. Then I shouted for Carla and the kids to witness this minor miracle.

I set Ethel down by the waterer, and she started drinking. For several minutes she continued to drink. She was really dehydrated. Her mood was odd, too. She didn't seem as perky as usual, which I attributed to the shock of being carried over the fence in a coyote's mouth.

Carla said, "Are you sure she's OK?"

"Yes," I said. "I checked her."

One of Carla's friends, who was also visiting, brushed some of Ethel's back feathers aside, revealing missing feathers and deep lacerations on her back and under her wings.

"Oh, no!" said Carla. "She's hurt. I'm calling the vet." She ran into the house. Ethel continued to gulp down water. When Carla came back, she said the vet wanted to see the bird right away. My sister-in-law, Melissa, took Ethel to the vet so I could finish building the enclosure.

Melissa returned with Ethel an hour and a half later. The vet had stapled up three deep bite wounds on the chicken's back, given her a dose of pain medication, and prescribed a tube of topical antibiotic. She still seemed to be in shock, warbling softly every few seconds. Melissa said the doctor gave her the option of an oral antibiotic but said that if we gave her oral antibiotics, her eggs would be inedible forever after. I didn't quite understand that—didn't the poultry industry regularly pump all sorts of antibiotics into chickens as a matter of course?

I consulted Google about eggs and antibiotics, and the only thing I could find was a discussion about it on a backyard chicken keepers' forum. People who had given antibiotics to their chickens said they simply waited a couple of weeks for the medicine to flush out of their chickens' systems and then resumed eating their eggs. Nevertheless, I decided to hold off on giving Ethel oral antibiotics unless she didn't respond well to the topical treatment.

Another thing we needed to figure out was where to keep Ethel while she was recuperating. The vet said that the other chickens would sense Ethel's weakness, attack her, and peck out her staples. We would have to keep them separated for at least a couple of weeks while her wounds healed. Fortunately, Melissa had a large, unused dog cage at her house, which was within walking distance of ours. I brought Ethel over, spread some wood shavings on the concrete floor of the cage, and gave her some food and water, which she consumed with relish. For the next two weeks, I would have to walk over to Melissa's twice a day, irrigate Ethel's wounds with a cleaning solution, and apply the antibiotic.

When I visited the next morning, Ethel seemed to be doing well. She was eating and had even laid an egg. By that night, she seemed to have slowed down a bit, but I attributed her sluggishness to the fact that chickens like to go to sleep early.

On Monday morning, Ethel didn't want to leave the pet carrier I'd placed in the cage to give her a place to sleep. I was able to bribe her out with a little cooked pasta, but she pecked at it listlessly. I called the vet and said I wanted the oral antibiotic. She was hesitant and again brought up the issue of the eggs. I told her I'd rather have her alive and producing nonedible eggs than dead.

I drove to the clinic. The receptionist made me sign a letter promising that I would forever keep Ethel separated from the other chickens and that I would never consume her eggs. He explained that the antibiotics would be transferred to the eggs, possibly resulting in health problems for anyone who consumed them.

I signed but with my fingers crossed behind my back. I still wasn't sure whether I was going to give her the medicine.

On Tuesday morning, Ethel was lying listlessly in the pet carrier. I called for her to come out, but she wouldn't get up. I gently removed her from the carrier and put her in my lap. After treating her wounds, I set her down; she stumbled and limped for a couple of feet, then stopped, unwilling to walk any farther. I decided it was time to give her the oral antibiotics.

The clinic told me to mix each dose into Ethel's feed. But she wasn't interested in eating her chicken scratch. My friend Shawn, who had a chicken that had survived an attack by an unknown woodland creature in northern California six months earlier, told me that she had put diced grapes into a large metal spoon mixed with the pink antibiotic and fed the mixture to her ailing hen. Since my hens loved grapes, I tried giving Ethel the same concoction, but she just knocked the grapes out of the spoon and didn't bother trying to eat them. I went back home and scrambled an egg—which my chickens love to eat more than anything else—and mixed that with a dose of antibiotic. She ate it with gusto.

But when I tried feeding her the egg-antibiotic cocktail again on Wednesday morning, she didn't want anything to do with it. I tried again with grapes, but no go. She had no appetite. I felt like I was losing her.

I was just about to call the clinic back when one of the vets called me to check up on Ethel's progress. When I explained her condition, the doctor told me to bring her in so she could show me how to squirt the antibiotic down Ethel's throat. "I have to show you, because it's easy to accidentally squirt it down her trachea and into her lungs," she said. "People have done that before."

I returned to my sister-in-law's house to fetch Ethel. She was back in the pet carrier, so I closed its door, picked it up, and drove her down the hill to the Studio City Animal Hospital. I was sent to a room, where a technician weighed Ethel, noting that she had lost about seventy grams since the last visit. That didn't seem like much to me, but the technician said it wasn't a good sign.

A little while later, Dr. Mao, the vet who had called me, came in. She seemed genuinely happy to see Ethel. She held the bird and moved the wings aside to examine the wounds. "They are healing really nicely!" she said. "That's good." Dr. Mao plucked out a few feathers that had gotten smeared into the wounds. Ethel flinched but didn't make too much of a fuss. The vet pulled aside Ethel's plumage with both hands to get a closer look at the bird's skin. "Oh, here's a laceration we missed," she said, pointing out a deep gash that ran for a couple of inches along the chicken's side. "We'll have to staple that up after I show you how to give her the antibiotic."

With her assistant holding Ethel, Dr. Mao pried open Ethel's beak and shined a flashlight down her throat. It was hard for me to see what was in there, besides her comically pointed tongue, but I caught a glimpse of a little slit that was opening and closing.

"That's where you *don't* want to give her the medicine," said Dr. Mao. "That's the opening to her trachea, called the epiglottis. If you put the syringe there, it'll deliver the medicine to her lungs."

"I don't see any other place to stick the syringe, though," I said. "Where's the throat hole?"

"It's hard to see," she said. "Let's take another look." She opened Ethel's beak again and aimed the flashlight down her throat. Ethel made a gasping sound. All I could see was a pink tube.

"The hole is kind of folded shut," she said. "That's why it's hard to see. Here, I'll give her some of the medicine, and you can watch me."

She filled the syringe with the pink antibiotic and pushed it into Ethel's open beak. Ethel kicked her legs and hissed. Moving the syringe to the right side of Ethel's epiglottis, Dr. Mao slid it in all the way to the handle. Then she pressed the plunger, delivering the full twenty-four-milliliter dose into Ethel's stomach. It felt good to know that Ethel was finally getting some antibiotics into her system.

"Now," Dr. Mao said, "I want you to try it." She filled the syringe with water from the sink and handed it to me. Her assistant was still holding Ethel. I opened her beak with one hand, but she jerked her head away and clamped her mouth shut. It's difficult to open a chicken's mouth when she doesn't want it to be opened, but I finally succeeded. I wedged my thumb and forefinger in the corner of her beak to prevent her from closing it again and stuck the syringe into the opening. Ethel gagged and struggled to break free, her legs scrabbling across the stainless-steel countertop.

I continued to push down on the syringe, frightened that I was going to hurt her. "Is that good?" I asked, ready to squirt the water.

"You have to push the syringe all the way down to the handle," she said. "Otherwise you can't be sure you've got it in the right place." I gently wiggled the syringe around and suddenly felt it slide effortlessly down until the entire thing was in her throat. I depressed the plunger, and all the water went into Ethel's stomach without any coming back up.

"Good!" said Dr. Mao. "You did it!" She was so nice and caring that I wished she could be my doctor. She took Ethel into another room, stapled the newly discovered wound, and gave her an intravenous injection of saline to rehydrate her.

I brought Ethel back to my sister-in-law's house and, twice a day for the next two weeks, I'd get on my bike, ride over, and squirt the medicine down the bird's throat. The first couple of times I brought Sarina along to hold Ethel down while I administered the medicine, but I eventually figured out a way to immobilize her between my knees so I could do it without assistance. Ethel never got used to the procedure, and as she started to improve, she got better at running away when I chased her around the cage. But I was always able to catch her and give her the medicine.

The oral antibiotics really did the trick. She started acting like the old Ethel after about four or five days, and her feathers started growing in, so she even looked like her former self. But she hadn't resumed laying eggs. That was probably because she was still on the mend internally. It didn't matter to me whether or not she'd ever lay eggs again. I was just happy to have her back.

I brought Ethel to the vet one more time, to have the staples removed. I was eager to return Ethel to her flock, because she looked lonely in the dog cage by herself. I was also getting a little tired of having to go to Melissa's every day. But the vet told me I shouldn't put Ethel in with the other chickens yet because they might pick at her staple holes. She should be sequestered for at least a week before reintroducing her to her friends.


## AN UNWELCOME HOMECOMING

Eight or nine days later, I put Ethel in her carrier and took her back to our house. What would the other chickens think of her after not seeing her for more than a month? Ethel had been the leader of the flock, so I hoped for the best. I opened the door to the chicken run and set the pet carrier inside. The other chickens, suspicious of the carrier, ran to the other side, eyeing it from a distance. I opened the carrier door, and Ethel tentatively stepped out. She went over to the food dispenser and began to eat. The other chickens, no longer afraid, approached her. In a few seconds they were mingling as if nothing had ever happened. But then Rosie, who had been the leader pro tempore during Ethel's absence, lunged at her. She jumped on Ethel's back and drove her beak between Ethel's wings, yanking out a tuft of feathers. Ethel squawked and ran to a corner. The other hens descended on her, clucking furiously. I had to run back in and grab Ethel to rescue her. The others were supremely agitated, letting loose long, sirenlike caws that were so loud they brought Carla out to see what all the fuss was about.

I explained what was going on, and she went back in the house to search Google for an answer. I sat on the ground and held Ethel in my lap, stroking her while the other chickens strutted around in a jerky manner. In a few minutes Carla came out. She didn't look happy. "Why didn't you research this first?" she said. "You're always shooting from the hip! You're supposed to keep Ethel separated by a fence in the run for a week so they can get used to one another. Now you'll have to take her back to my sister's while you make a new fence."

I didn't want to make a new fence. I'd promised Carla that I would help her unpack the moving boxes that had been cluttering the house for weeks. The chickens had kept me so busy that I hadn't been much help with getting settled in the new house. I felt like I'd spent more time with the chickens in the last six weeks than with my wife and daughters. Was this worth three or four eggs a day?

A fence would take too much time to build. I thought about the quickest way to take care of the problem. I looked at the roll of wire mesh next to the coop. "OK," I said. "I can divide the chicken run into two areas with this wire-mesh fence. It'll only take ten minutes or so." I quickly set up a separating wall inside the chicken run, securing it with cable ties. I put Ethel on her side, gave her some food and water, and placed the pet carrier in there to give her a place to sleep. The other chickens were furious with the new arrangement and ran back and forth along the new barrier looking for a way to breach it so they could peck Ethel some more. Ethel aloofly ignored the irate hens, eating and drinking from her personal food and water containers.

Now that Ethel was safe from the other chickens, I left her alone and went into the house to help Carla unpack. I forgot about Ethel until evening, when we were ready to go to bed. I went outside with a flashlight and found her sitting on top of the pet carrier. Its door had swung shut, so she had been unable to get inside to sleep. I crawled into the pen and put Ethel in the carrier. I didn't lock the door, thinking she might get claustrophobic if she couldn't get out. I just swung the door closed, figuring she'd push it open in the morning.

When I woke up the next day, I checked on Ethel and found her still in the pet carrier. I propped the door open with a stick, and she came out and started drinking water. She was parched. I decided I'd better keep the pet carrier door open at night so she wouldn't get stuck inside again.

That night, after putting the kids to bed, I went into the spare bedroom I used as an office to check my e-mail, and Carla went into the bedroom to read. After a few minutes she came into the office and whispered urgently, "It sounds like someone is walking around right next to the bedroom!"

"I'll check," I said. Carla handed me the aluminum baseball bat we keep for self-defense, and I grabbed the flashlight I keep on my nightstand. I shined the light through the glass door and didn't see anything, at least not at first. Then, over by the chicken coop, I saw what looked like a couple of candle lights. They flickered, went out, and then reappeared.

"I see something!" I hissed. "Some little lights back there." I pointed them out to Carla.

"What are they?" she said.

It struck me that they must be reflections from a wild animal's eyes.

"Oh, no!" I said. "An animal is trying to get the chickens."

I opened the door and kept my flashlight trained on the shining eyes. They disappeared. I walked hesitantly toward the coop. Did mountain lions live in these hills? I know they have been spotted in Los Angeles before. I felt ridiculous walking out there, barefoot with a pencil flashlight and a baseball bat in the pitch dark with no idea what kind of enemy I might be facing. I swept the light around the property and caught the shining eyes again, this time closer to the fence that separated our yard from the undeveloped canyon below. My flashlight wasn't strong enough for me to make out what kind of animal was down there, but from the vague, roundish outline, it didn't seem like a coyote. If I had to guess, I'd say it was a raccoon. I kept the flashlight on it, thumped the bat on the ground, and yelled for the animal to go away. The eyes disappeared.

I turned the light to the chicken run. Ethel wasn't in the pet carrier. She wasn't in the pen. Then I saw the wooden stakes I'd used to hold down the wire mesh. They'd been ripped out of the ground. One of the stakes was smeared a shiny red. I saw feathers scattered next to the pen.

"It got Ethel!" I shouted to Carla, who was standing in the bedroom doorway.

"Oh, no!" she said. When I got back to the bedroom, she hugged me and told me how sorry she was. I suddenly felt exhausted and foolish. Everything I'd done to help Ethel get better had been a waste of time. After weeks of medical care and recuperation, a hungry predator had snatched her in a flash, and that was the end of her.

# DO I DESERVE TO KEEP CHICKENS?

That night, Carla and I talked about our eight months with the chickens. In our old house, the hens had had the run of the yard and had been supremely happy. It was a pleasure to watch them graze, take naps on the wrought-iron table in the front yard, chase squirrels, and mingle with our cats (who pretended the chickens weren't there). We'd never seen a coyote, and while we'd seen raccoons once in a while, they'd never bothered the chickens.

But raising chickens here in Studio City had stopped being fun, both for us and for the chickens. During the day they were constrained to an area off to the side of the house, so we weren't able to enjoy their presence in the way that we had when we lived in the old house. Here the wildlife was fiercer and bolder. My attempt to build a predator-free environment for them had put a strain on my family, because I'd spent so much time on it. The chickens laid eggs less frequently than before, the yolks weren't as orange as they had been, and the hens had picked up the habit of pecking and breaking the eggs in the nest box. The fun we'd had with the chickens had been spoiled.

While conducting my DIY experiments, I'd been telling myself that it was OK to make mistakes, but when the lives of animals, particularly ones you've grown fond of, are lost as a result, it's not OK. And when DIY takes you away from your family, it defeats the purpose, at least as I've been defining it. DIY is supposed to be rewarding and enriching and communal, not stressful and isolating.

Having lost two chickens, I considered what to do next. I wondered whether I even deserved to have chickens. Carla said that we had to consider the new environment we lived in and do the kinds of things that worked *with* it instead of fighting against it. The makeshift chicken pen I'd slapped together after the coyote attack was an example of fighting against the environment. The pen was an attempt to keep out the things that were surrounding it. Keeping chickens here would be an endless struggle, fraught with chronic, low-grade anxiety that a predator was digging its way in.

Why not refocus on vegetable gardening, Carla suggested, and growing an orchard of exotic fruits on the hillside? She pointed out that I'd had a great time gardening the year before, and she was right. We didn't have a large, flat area for a garden in our new house, but we had a big deck that got a lot of sunlight and would be a perfect place to put some self-watering containers.

"We could give the chickens away to someone who has a better place for them," said Carla. I liked the idea. It wasn't fair to keep them here. They needed a place where they could scratch and roam freely. I called the people living in our Tarzana house and asked if they'd be interested in keeping our four remaining chickens. They said they would be happy to take them as soon as they got back from vacation a few weeks later. I told them I'd call them at that time so we could make arrangements for me to come over with the chickens and give them a few lessons on how to keep them.

But when the end of June rolled around, I didn't call the tenants. I just kept tending to the chickens as usual. Carla didn't mention our plans either. I suspect neither of us really wanted to live without chickens.

In November, we were down to two hens, having lost Rosie and Daisy in August to a predator who grabbed them when they'd escaped into a part of our yard that didn't have a fence. The two remaining chickens, Jordan and Darla, were always the shyest of the bunch. Maybe it pays for a chicken to be fearful, with so many other animals (including humans) salivating at the sight of them. Darla has taken to spending her days in the nesting box, leaving only for a moment to eat and drink, then scurrying back to her dark cubbyhole. A visitor who keeps chickens told me that Darla is "broody." Hens that are broody want to sit on a clutch of eggs and do little else. They make a strange growl if you get too close to them. She told me to lock Darla out of the coop. I've been keeping her out during the day, but at night I have to put her back in to keep the coyotes away. One Web site suggests keeping a "very active young cockerel" in the pen to cure a hen of broodiness. "He just won't let them sit there as he'll constantly be trying to mate them." I don't want a rooster, so I might try the other suggestion offered: putting some ice cubes under her while she's nesting.

Even though keeping chickens can be difficult and at times discouraging and frustrating, there's something wonderful about having them around. Humans and chickens have been living with each other for ten thousand years, and it's a bond that's hard to break. Carla wants me to build a bigger coop, with a nicer-looking pen. I'm glad she wants to keep chickens. Raising these fascinating animals, despite all the hassles involved, is one of the most rewarding experiences I've ever had. Now that we have chickens in our life, we don't want to go back to living without them.

# 6 STRUMMING AND STIRRING

"What's important about this making stuff is that it's a balance to what I call 'digeritis,' which is having everything virtual and electronic. When you make things by hand, it's yours; there's no mystery how it got made. If you get an idea and you make it yourself, there's something about that that is really good for you."
—JAY BALDWIN, A LONGTIME EDITOR AT
*WHOLE EARTH CATALOG*

Twenty-five years ago, a guitar maker from Minneapolis named Bob McNally designed a stringed musical instrument that even a rank amateur could use to make sweet-sounding music. He called it the Strumstick. With its triangular body and three strings, it resembled a small Russian balalaika. Today McNally sells Strumsticks (generically known as stick dulcimers) on his Web site for $140. The instrument uses drone, or diatonic, tuning, in which the frets are spaced to give only the major notes of the scale. Mountain dulcimers, bagpipes, and sitars use this tuning as well. To make music with a Strumstick, all you have to do is press down on any fret along the neck and strum all three strings. The unfretted strings will accompany the fretted string with pleasing harmony. I've owned one for a couple of years, and it's a hit with visitors who've never learned to play a guitar, because making nice sounds with the Strumstick is foolproof.

One day in 2008 as I was strumming, I started wondering if anyone had made his own Strumstick. I looked for videos on You-Tube and found plenty of people who had made their own drone-tuned instruments. Some had used cigar boxes for the body, and the resulting instruments looked and sounded great. I thought this might be a fun way to make my own stick dulcimer, but the frets intimidated me. You needed to saw grooves into the neck and insert the metal frets, all at the same height and in such a way that they wouldn't pop out. I couldn't find any good information online about installing frets, so I put the idea aside.

A couple of weeks later, I stumbled across a Web site that dem-onstrated how to make a ukulele out of a Tupperware container. It wasn't pretty, but it sounded great. More impressive, at least to me, was how the guy made the frets for it—with flat toothpicks. He sim-ply glued them along the neck at the proper locations with epoxy. Suddenly, the barrier to entry had been lowered enough for me to give instrument making a try. I ordered a set of ukulele tuning pegs ($8) and a set of baritone ukulele strings ($6), and when they arrived a couple of days later, I went to work.

First, I needed some wood for the neck and body. I didn't have a cigar box handy, but since I planned to make the instrument electric, I could use a solid piece of wood. Sifting through my scrap-lumber collection didn't turn up anything usable, but when I examined the clubhouse my daughters had built in the backyard, I found a piece of wood attached to it, originally from a kitchen table that had broken a couple of years earlier, that looked like it might do the trick. I pried it loose. (I caught flak for it when Sarina noticed the missing piece of her clubhouse a couple of days later.)

Using my Strumstick as a guide, I measured the length of the strings from the bridge to the nut, adding about six more inches. That way, I could make the neck and the body out of a single piece of wood, eliminating the need for fasteners and glue.

To mark where the frets would go, I just held the Strumstick up against my piece of wood and made marks with a pencil. Then I used a jigsaw to cut the wood to size and sanded it smooth.

All the little problems to be addressed in making the stick dulcimer had me scurrying to different parts of the house, the scrap pile, and even the trash can in search of solutions. It felt great to be so engaged with what I was doing, using my hands and mind together to make a physical object instead of just moving a mouse around and tapping keys to interface with the world of bits (which is how I spent the majority of my waking hours). Getting involved with something tactile that demands concentration, observation, and resourcefulness was exhilarating.

After coming up with a way to attach the tuners to the end of the neck, I glued down wooden matchsticks—I had forgotten to buy toothpicks—on the penciled-in fret marks. In twenty minutes, the epoxy was dry enough to string the instrument and tune it for a test strum. To my surprise, it worked! It was much quieter than the Strumstick, since the strings were nylon instead of steel and it didn't have a hollow resonating box. But it was a real, working three-stringed instrument. I tried different fret positions, and they all sounded good.

Next, I needed to electrify my instrument by adding a pickup. Most acoustic-guitar players use a microphone with a suction cup that attaches to the guitar's body, but makers of cigar-box guitars typically either hand-wind their own electric pickups or use a piezoelectric buzzer. This is the component in a smoke alarm that makes that awful high-pitched whine at the first sign of burnt toast, but it can also be used as a microphone. I didn't happen to have an unused smoke alarm sitting around, but Radio Shack sells the buzzers for a few bucks. I already had one in my junk drawer, and after a lot of experimenting, I ended up cracking open the black plastic housing and removing the paper-thin, nickel-sized metal disc that was the piezoelectric component.

I hollowed out a space in the body for the patch-cord jack and the buzzer. I used a wooden Tinkertoy hub to cover up the hole in the front of the instrument. I had hoped it would look neat, especially since the patch cord would be inserted in the hole in the center of the Tinkertoy hub. But it ended up looking cheap and badly proportioned. Carla said it ruined the simplicity of the design. I agreed. It would have been better to have hollowed out the space for the buzzer from the back of the body and just have a simple hole in the front for the patch cord. Now I had to somehow fix my mistake. I removed the Tinkertoy and rummaged through drawers and boxes looking for something that would work. I spotted a wooden yardstick in a closet. I cut off a small piece, drilled a hole through it for the jack, and glued it to the body of the stick dulcimer (or dronestick, as my friend Steve Lodefink called it when I e-mailed him a photo of the completed instrument), covering the gouged-out hollow. It looked good! The mistake had forced me to come up with something that turned out better than I could have planned.

I finished up the dronestick just in time to take it with me for my appearance on *The Martha Stewart Show* in New York. I was invited to demonstrate some of the cool DIY projects we featured in the magazine (including the temperature-control system for my espresso machine). It was surreal to see Martha pick the instrument up and play it in front of a national audience of TV viewers. Unfortunately, I forgot to ask her to sign it for me.

A few days after building my dronestick, Steve Lodefink (a Leonardo da Vinci of the broad-spectrum hobbyist world, who makes everything from high-flying water rockets to realistic *Planet of the Apes* suits and blogs about his creations at finkbuilt.com) sent me a photo of a handsome cigar-box guitar he had built, and I posted it to Boing Boing. A commenter who goes by the handle ZombyWoof wrote:

> *I don't get it. Ukes I can live with, they're a legitimate instrument, but these things simply sound bad due to the poor resonance. It looks very well done for what it is, but if you want to scratch a Make/DIY itch I would do some other project and just buy an inexpensive used guitar to play.*

ZombyWoof had a point. A used guitar with a nice sound doesn't cost a lot. But you'd miss the joy of playing an instrument you've made with your own hands. The folks who hang out at Cigar Box Nation, a Web site for home guitar makers, know all about this feeling of satisfaction. The site has photos and videos of all kinds of ingeniously made stringed instruments, posted by their builders. I was drawn to the music of a guy who goes by the handle One String Willie. He makes crude one-string instruments called diddley bows, which were invented by African slaves in America and were probably based on a similar African musical instrument that required two musicians to play.

After watching his videos, I concluded that One String Willie was a tough, grim character, with his opaque aviator sunglasses and black wool cap pulled down over his head. But I learned that he is also a research chemist for a large pharmaceutical firm in Pennsylvania. His name is David Williams, and after we struck up a correspondence, he sent me one of his terrific CDs, *A Store Bought Guitar Just Won't Do*, which has songs by both Williams (on a four-string cigar-box guitar of his own making) and his alter ego, Willie (on a one-string diddley bow). The CD cover has side-by-side photos of Williams and Willie, and I was surprised to see how non-menacing he looked in real life. The first song on the CD was titled "A Different Guitar," and it was about how much he loved his handmade four-string cigar-box guitar.

I figured Williams would have something to say about Zomby-Woof's disdain for homemade instruments. I called him up. "Do you think store-bought instruments sound better?" I asked.

"*Better* is the wrong word," he said. "It sounds 'different,' not better." Besides, he said, the joy of creation is reason enough to build your own musical instrument. On his Web site (www .onestringwillie.com), Williams mentions Ralph Waldo Emerson's essay "Self-Reliance." Williams explained that Emerson believed "society tends to push people toward conformity, and while conformity is OK in many areas of life, like following traffic laws or wiring your house correctly, it is less welcome in other areas, such as the arts. A homemade instrument allows—*forces*—you to break out of the rut of artistic conformity, as there is no established way of playing, there is no established way the instrument is expected to sound, and there are no books to tell you how to proceed. You need to teach yourself how to make music come out of your homemade instrument, drawing from your experiences with other instruments and from the music that is inside your head. If you view this as a journey and not a destination, it is a liberating and joyful experience."

Another important reason to make your own instrument, Williams told me, is that doing so breaks you out of the mind-set that musicians (and, really, everybody else) have that buying the latest gear will make you happier. Before he started constructing didley bows and cigar-box guitars, Williams would enter a music store thinking that if he bought a new guitar or accessory, he'd become a better player. "But after building my own instrument for little more than the list price of a CD, I realized that I didn't need an expensive guitar to express myself or to entertain myself or an audience. Building and playing a homemade instrument helps the guitarist to avoid lusting after the latest and greatest gear and to focus on really learning to play on the instrument they have. This runs contrary to the mainstream music industry, which works to drive the lust to buy things."

This, of course, is an example of the kind of marketing that Edward Bernays created in the early twentieth century. Marketers are constantly pushing new features of consumer electronics and other products as a way to get people to throw away perfectly good stuff and spend money on new versions with faster speeds, smaller packages, more megapixels, greater range, lighter weight, bigger displays, more memory. The truth is, the stuff we already own is loaded with features most of us haven't learned to use. But people are beginning to get wise to this. In April 2009, Web entrepreneur Anil Dash launched a Web site called Last Year's Model (www.lastyearsmodel.org), which runs testimonials from people who've learned to enjoy the older techno-gadgets they already own.

Dash encourages people to send Twitter messages about the way they use trailing-edge technology. Some examples: "My 1st generation iPod mini still plays my songs," wrote apatino331. "My 2003 Pentium 4 runs Photoshop and Illustrator CS2 . . . AT THE SAME TIME! WOO!" wrote jusuzuki. "Using a 4 year old Sony Cell phone, and damned proud of it! Resist the shiny new toys!" wrote janoallen. "I've just repaired my 14 year old CD player, upgraded the parts in my G5 iMac and am hanging onto my old mobile phone," wrote laceybloke. "Old skool."

Even though these folks are tweeting about stuff they bought (as opposed to stuff they made themselves), the same idea applies. In fact, making stuff takes the idea one step further. Using cast-off technology to make something new is a way to experience the fun of having something new while getting more use out of old stuff that would have been discarded.

# MY THREE-STRINGED ADDICTION

I had so much fun building my stick dulcimer (and playing it for everyone I could corner) that I wanted to make more stringed instruments. The happy enthusiasts at the Cigar Box Nation Web site were very encouraging. Anytime I had a question about building a cigar-box guitar, I'd have a helpful answer within minutes. As a rule, DIYers will go out of their way to help one another succeed.

I went to work on my next instrument, this time using a real cigar box I picked up at a cigar store near my house. I made plenty of mistakes: For the neck I used the same kitchen-table pine, which was weathered and split easily, forcing me to use glue to keep it together. The slots I cut for the frets were crooked; and I didn't allow for the thickness of the box lid, so the fret board was too low, causing the strings to buzz on the higher frets. As the mistakes piled up, I came close to abandoning the project and starting over but then decided that this would be my practice cigar-box guitar. I was going to complete it and not worry about the mistakes, learning from them so I could avoid making the same mistakes on subsequent guitars. This turns out to be a best practice for DIY. Finishing the job, no matter how botched, will wring the most knowledge out of the experience and lead to better results the next time a similar project is tackled.

It took a couple of weeks to finish the guitar, and despite its many flaws, it played well and sounded surprisingly good. It turns out that cigar-box guitars are forgiving instruments. The sound was clear, and the amplification worked wonderfully. The only real problem was the buzzing sound the strings made when I went past the twelfth fret, so I sanded down part of the lid and was able to go a few frets higher. Shane Speal, a cofounder of Cigar Box Nation, saw a photo of my guitar that I posted along with my description of all its faults, and he commented, "And yet, all those imperfections make it a perfect cigar box guitar. Welcome to your new addiction, Mark!"

With two stringed instruments under my belt, I was more excited than ever to build another one. I'd picked up skills and confidence along the way (I no longer dreaded installing metal frets— what had I been so afraid of?), and there were new things I wanted to try. I started making a list of all the kinds of instruments I wanted to build—a stand-up bass, a cookie-tin ukulele, a banjo, a fretless four-stringer. I daydreamed about the different kinds of paint jobs I could give them and the materials I could use to make them.

For my next cigar-box guitar, I bought a six-foot length of one-by-two oak from Home Depot. I made sure it was flat and straight. It weighed a lot more than the pine I'd used in my first guitar and felt a lot better in my hands. I also bought a small metal miter box from a hobby store to cut the fret slots in the neck. This time I made perfectly straight fret cuts.

To avoid the buzzing-string problem I had encountered with my first cigar-box guitar, I shaved off the part of the neck that attached to the cigar box, so that the surface of the fret board was flush with the top of the cigar box. Remembering Mister Jalopy's dictum "Screws, not glues," I screwed the neck to the box with three fasteners. That way, if I needed to make changes or later wanted to use a new cigar box for the body, it would be a simple matter to separate the two parts.

I made a couple of small mistakes, like drilling a hole in a spot that hit a screw going in a perpendicular direction to the hole, but this guitar build went faster and more smoothly than the previous one. The action was low, but not so low that it buzzed, and I could play the strings up to the twentieth fret without interference. When I sent photos to Mister Jalopy and Steve Lodefink, they gave me the thumbs-up.

As of this writing, I've built five guitars. Making guitars has become a passion of mine. I've given some of them as gifts, and the recipients have been delighted (or at least kind enough to pretend to be). Not a day goes by that I fail to either pick up one of my instruments and play a few licks or think about what I'm going to do on my next build. Building cigar-box guitars has allowed me to touch the core of handmade happiness.

## A STIRRING PASSION

Having grown comfortable using tools to make things out of wood, I decided to try something even simpler than guitars—wooden kitchen implements. Starting off with spoons seemed like a good idea. I already own spoons for cooking, of course, but I'd never paid attention to them. I pulled them out of the drawer to look at them, really look, for the first time. They were for the most part cheap, ugly things. The wood had a rough, almost fuzzy surface texture that I found unappealing to touch.

I had read that cherry wood was a good choice for first-time carvers. It just so happened that I had a large branch from an ornamental plum tree in our backyard. That should be close enough, I figured. It had broken off during a windy day a couple of months earlier, and I was planning on cutting it up into pieces and stuffing them into the trash. It wasn't a task I looked forward to, so I put it off. Eventually, Sarina lodged it between the living branches of the cherry tree as part of a tent. Seeing the branch every time I walked by gave me a pang of procrastinator's guilt. But now I could do something fun with the branch. Suddenly it went from being a piece of trash to a source of valuable raw material. This wasn't a unique occurrence: Ever since jumping into the DIY world, I had found this happening more and more. Stuff I used to throw away—rubber hoses with holes, pieces of chain, electrical cords, scraps of lumber—became useful parts for projects. When life hands you lemons, make lemonade. When it hands you a broken tree branch, make a wooden spoon.

The branch was about six feet long, fairly straight, and about two and a half inches in diameter. It had a somewhat oval, rather than circular, cross-section. It was easy to cut a twelve-inch length using a pruning saw. But when I tried the same saw to make a lengthwise cut (to get a rectangular slice from which to carve a spoon), I ran into problems. I held the section upright in one hand while sawing with the other. The arrangement was unstable; I couldn't hold the piece of wood steady enough for the teeth to dig into the wood. The saw blade would just jump off the top. The blades were spaced too far apart for this kind of work. I found my miter saw and tried that, bracing the branch against a fence post with my leg. It was an awkward and dangerous setup, but the saw finally started cutting a groove in the wood.

Sawing lengthwise was slow going, though. The wood was very hard, unlike the pine I'd used for my chicken shack. My arm was getting tired, and I'd only cut into the wood about half an inch. This would take forever. Before giving up, though, I decided to try one more thing—splitting the log lengthwise. I didn't have much hope for success, since (1) I didn't own a log splitter and (2) I'd never split a log before. Nevertheless, I pulled out my Fubar (a hammerlike tool that had come in handy when I tore apart the paint shack to build my chicken coop) and inserted its wedge end into the shallow groove I'd managed to cut into one end of the log. I tapped the Fubar with a hammer, driving the wedge down. To my amazement, I was able to cleave the wood with little effort. I ended up with a fine piece of stock for making my spoon.

I had a brand-new pocketknife with a sharp blade. This is what I planned to use to whittle my spoon. But I discovered that it was useless on this hard wood. I might as well have been using a butter knife to carve granite. When I researched the art of spoon carving online, the instructions I found referred to special kinds of knives and gouges. Shuffling around my toolbox, hoping to find something that could work, I came across a cheap plastic utility knife, the kind with little blades that you can snap off when they get dull. I tried it out on the wood, and it whittled off shavings quite well. I put on a pair of leather work gloves, sat down in a rocking chair on the front porch, and began whittling in earnest.

─ ─ ─ ─ ─ ─ ─ ─ ─

I'm a fidgeter by nature. I feel better when I have something to do with my hands. I often keep a lump of rubber artist's eraser or Silly Putty at my desk to give me something to do while I'm on the phone, or else I'll start surfing the Web or checking e-mail, which makes my attention drift away from the conversation. But an activity like whittling satisfies my urge to fidget without affecting the part of my brain needed to pay attention to people who are talking to me. I've noticed that if I play music while I write or read, I literally cannot hear the music—I just shut it out. But if I'm drawing or painting, I can listen to music, talk on the phone, or hold a conversation with another person in the room. Whittling, to me, is like drawing or painting. My mind can wander but far more pleasantly than if I were just sitting there with nothing to do.

According to Dr. Herbert Benson, the founder and president of the Benson-Henry Institute for Mind Body Medicine at

Massachusetts General Hospital, the repetitive aspect of knitting elicits a "relaxation response," which results in lowered heart rate, blood pressure, metabolism, and muscle tension. I suspect that whittling and knitting have similar effects on the brain and body.

In another study, Andrea Price, a knitting-book author, got together with her brother, Eric Miller, a biofeedback practitioner and researcher, to measure the relaxation response of knitting. In their self-produced video, Price explained that she was "struck by the common wisdom that says knitting is a soothing activity," but when she looked around online, she couldn't find research that supported that belief. Price enlisted her brother to conduct a "simple experiment right here in his living room."

Miller attached a sensor to his sister's finger. The sensor was connected to a computer that displayed Price's heart rate and galvanic skin response (which correlates with the intensity of a person's emotional state). Price was not allowed to see the screen as she knitted. To get baseline numbers, Miller had her sit quietly in a chair for a little while. (While Price sat, Miller's dog came over and began licking her fingers. Wisely, Dr. Miller removed the dog, stating that its presence might affect the results.) After a couple of minutes, Miller asked his sister to start knitting. Almost immediately, her heart rate and galvanic skin response began to drop. Through knitting alone, Price's average heart rate dropped from 91.45 to 85.64 beats per minute, and her galvanic skin response went from 68.49 to 63.90.

- - - - - - - - -

My three-hour whittling session on the porch—interrupted occasionally by conversation with my family and watching my chickens engage in an entertaining (and fortunately bloodless) turf war with a foolhardy squirrel—was marvelous. It was the opposite of Web surfing, where my eyes dance over the pages without reading anything deeply and my mouse finger itches to click on the next hyperlink. As I whittled away without a plan, the rough outline of a spoon began to take shape before my eyes. I felt as though I were revealing the hidden spoon within the wood by removing the superfluous material surrounding it. (This is what Michelangelo said of sculpting: he was freeing the figures from the marble.) A sizable pile of curled shavings accumulated at my feet. The muscles in my right arm burned but in a way that didn't bother me, at least not enough to snap me out of my whittling reverie. I was having too much fun to stop.

Eventually, I had what looked very much like a spoon, except for the hollowed-out part. From my research, I knew there were a number of ways to form the hollow. I could use a hook knife or a gouge; or I could chip away at the bowl with a knife until I had a rough concave shape, then use a blunt stick wrapped in sandpaper to smooth it out.

I went to the local craft store to buy a wood-carving set. The only thing they carried was a five-dollar kit containing five wood-handled carving tools. I bought it and took it home. The U-shaped gouge that came with it worked surprisingly well, considering how cheap it was. Using it to carve the hollow of the spoon was a little like scooping out hard-frozen ice cream from a container. I took care not to make the concave part so deep that it would break through to the other side. The gouge left a lot of little channels in the surface, which I smoothed out with sandpaper.

A light overall sanding was all that was needed to complete the project. I didn't try to give the spoon a mirror finish. I liked the rough-hewn look of the final product, with its thick handle and the easily discernible whittling planes that composed a mosaic of small facets across its surface. I hefted it in my hand and pretended to stir a hearty stew. The spoon felt solid and capable of handling the most viscous of pancake batters. I was proud of my creation. This spoon, which had been hiding inside that broken branch for the last couple of months, was now a tool I'd use daily for many years (or so I hoped).

When I showed my spoon to Carla, she was genuinely impressed. I gave it a light coat of canola oil to make the grain stand out, wiped it down, and added it to the widemouthed jar on the kitchen counter with the soon-to-be-replaced cooking implements.

A couple of days later I went to work on a second spoon. This time, I wanted to make something a little more shapely and streamlined. I started with a thinner section of wood and used a wood rasp to quickly shave the outline. I was on a long conference call while I worked on it, so I kept the phone on mute most of the time while I noisily scraped and carved. I was able to pay attention to the conversation while I worked; in fact, I paid more attention to the conversation than I would have if I hadn't been doing anything with my hands. The calming and focusing effect of spoon whittling is nothing short of miraculous.

By the time the call was over, I was ready to hollow out the scoop end of the spoon. I got the gouger and started cutting with it, but it was a lot duller than before. I wasn't surprised. What should I expect from a $1 tool? At this point I could have used my Dremel tool (a motorized drill-like device to which you can attach different kinds of cutting, grinding, sharpening, drilling, and polishing bits) to hollow out the scoop part, but if I resorted to power tools, I might lose the relaxation response I got from whittling. It would speed things up too much for my liking. However, using the Dremel to sharpen the *gouge* seemed far enough removed from the process of carving that I figured it wouldn't adulterate the purity of the experience.

The Dremel tool spins so fast that it screams when you use it. The grinding bit I used easily cut into the metal of the gouge. But when I tried the gouge on the spoon, it was as bad as before. Either I wasn't getting the right angle for sharpening or the gouge was just such a piece of junk that the metal was no good. I went online and found a large number of pages and videos about sharpening gouges. It turns out that sharpening is just the first step in maintaining a gouge. You also have to hone and polish it. From what I picked up, honing and polishing are really just refined sharpening.

I put my spoon away until I could get a proper gouge and the tools needed to keep it sharp. I ordered a No. 10 Bent 8mm gouge for $24.50 from Woodcraft.com, along with a sharpening kit for $13.99. The scoop-shaped blade of the gouge was as shiny as a mirror. I had no idea how sharp it was until I put the piece of wood I was whittling in my lap and started using the gouge. It slipped off the wood, jabbed a hole through my pants, and left a U-shaped cut in my thigh.

I started whittling over a table after that.

After making several spoons for use in the kitchen, I made one as a present for Sarina's art teacher. Because it was a gift, I wanted to make it larger than usual, with a deeper scoop. I split off another piece of my log (I still had most of it!) and started whittling. Some days I'd spend ten or fifteen minutes on it; other days I hacked away for an hour or more. The spoon emerged from the wood without much in the way of conscious direction on my part. What would it end up looking like? I had no idea. I enjoy the surprise aspect.

As I dug away at the scoop of the spoon, I ran into a problem. The center of the branch was hollow. A tiny tunnel ran through the entire branch. This caused an ugly hole to appear in three parts of the spoon—at the front and back of the hollow part and near the end of the handle. I'd been working on the spoon for over a week, and now this. Was I going to have to chuck the whole thing and start over? Before I did that, I decided to try to patch it up. I collected the sawdust that had accumulated on the table from sanding the spoon and mixed it with a little wood glue, forming a putty. I pushed as much of the putty as I could into the holes and let it dry. The putty was noticeably darker after drying, but I convinced myself that it gave the spoon a certain ramshackle-solid charm. I gave the spoon a final sanding and applied a polish made from beeswax and olive oil.

I showed the spoon to Carla. She loved it. "I think you should make a spoon for everyone we need to give a gift to," she said. I liked that idea, too. The trouble was, it took at least five hours to make a spoon, so I couldn't make enough unless I spent every hour of every weekend making them. The other option would be to use power tools to rough out the shape of the spoons, and then use hand tools to finish them. But I didn't want to do that. I felt that if I went down that path, I'd miss out on the very reason I had started making spoons in the first place. I would just have to be OK with making as many spoons as I made. I didn't want this hobby to become a stressful job instead of a source of joy and relief.

Making something as humble as a wooden spoon doesn't count as much of an artistic achievement. It's nothing compared to the work of, say, the master carvers of the misnamed "Black Forest" school, a group of Victorian-era Swiss artists who carved incredibly detailed life-sized bears and other animals, music boxes, furniture, and astounding three-dimensional reproductions of famous paintings, such as Leonardo da Vinci's *Last Supper*. Of course, I'm envious of artists and craftsmen who are far more skilled and dedicated than I am at making things of beauty. They put my meager efforts to shame. But I try to accept my limitations and realize that by whittling my own spoons, I've gained the following:

**1. New appreciation for masterful woodwork and sculpture.** Now that I know how much effort and skill go into carving, I'm more interested in studying the work of artists who use wood in their art. I notice things about their work that I wouldn't have before I started whittling. Making your own stuff is one of the best ways to enhance your powers of observation and subsequently your appreciation of what's around you. And learning to appreciate the work of masters has also helped me to appreciate my own, much more modest efforts and inspired me to experiment with new techniques and styles.

**2. Control of my environment.** I'm happy to do the best I can, even if that is just an asymmetrical wooden spoon. Whatever flaws and features the spoon possesses are a result of my efforts. I can learn from my mistakes and try to do better next time. This kind of control is impossible if you buy everything you need. It's nice to know that there are plenty of opportunities to improve as I continue to whittle.

**3. A connection with other people.** Sarina's art teacher's response to getting the spoon was better than I'd hoped. She was delighted with it and actually liked the darker putty patches just as I did. I enjoy showing my spoons to visitors, and they are interested—or at least are polite enough to pretend to be—in them. The spoons are conversation pieces, and they trigger interesting memories in the people who see them. Some have recalled their grandfathers' woodcraft projects or their childhood whittling activities.

Now that I've gained some experience making spoons, chicken coops, and cigar-box guitars, basic woodworking is no longer as mysterious as it once was. I know much more about the peculiar-ities of wood—how it splits, warps, fights back, and acquiesces to my attempts to make something new out of it. I know more about what to look for when picking out lumber. From the few projects I've completed, my attitude about making things of all kinds—planning, designing, and building them—has improved. I feel like I've tuned in to a better way of living.

# 7 FOMENTING FERMENTATION

In 1995 Carla's mother, Jackie, told me about the batches of "mushroom tea" she had been making from a self-reproducing blob of fungus. One of her clients (Jackie owned a tax-preparing business) had given her the mushroom, telling her that its origins went back hundreds of years to Russia. Jackie said the brew was called *kombucha*; it was supposed to restore health to the drinker. In fact, she said, it was a cure-all.

The next time Carla and I visited Jackie, she led us to her dining room. A one-gallon glass bowl sat on the table, covered with a square of thin white cloth. She lifted the cloth to reveal a milky-tan gelatinous disk the size of a dinner plate floating on the surface of light amber tea. "That's the mushroom," she said. It looked like an alien lifeform, a slimy blob with what appeared to be veins running through it.

Jackie said it was time to harvest this particular batch of tea, as it had been fermenting for a week. She washed her hands and transferred the blob, dripping with tea and sporting a few brown mucousy tendrils, to a plate. The smell of vinegar wafted up from the bowl. She ladled the tea into a glass jar and asked if we wanted to try it. Feeling adventurous, Carla and I assented. Jackie ladled some into glasses and handed them to us. I took a sip, expecting it to have a funky, moldy flavor, but it was crisp and fizzy, like spar-kling apple cider mixed with a little vinegar. I asked for more.

"I can give you a mushroom if you want to make it yourself," Jackie said. I told her I'd like that. She picked up the mushroom that was on the plate and pointed out that there were really two mushrooms stuck together. "It creates a new mushroom with each batch of tea you make," she said. She peeled them apart and put my mushroom in a Ziploc plastic bag with an ounce or two of the tea to keep it moist. She also gave me the simple recipe: "Steep six to eight black tea bags in a gallon of water. Remove the tea bags. Add one cup of sugar. Pour the sugared tea into a glass container. Place the *kombucha* mushroom on top of the tea. Cover with cloth and let it ferment for a week. Enjoy!"

I took my adopted mushroom home and followed the recipe; it worked without a hitch. I was surprised by how automatic the pro-cess was. I just set up the initial conditions and let nature take over. I went online to find out more about *kombucha,* but there was pre-cious little information about it at the time.

I didn't think much about the purported health benefits of *kom-bucha*—I drank it for the taste. And after a few months, Carla and I moved, and I never got around to starting the process up again. By that time, my mother-in-law had lost interest in *kombucha,* too.

I pretty much forgot about the fermented treat until a few years ago, when commercial versions of *kombucha* started showing up in places like Whole Foods. The Web was now awash with informa-tion about it. I learned that the blob isn't really a mushroom at all but, rather, a "symbiotic culture of bacteria and yeast," affection-ately known as a SCOBY.

The history of *kombucha* is unclear. One book says it originated in Southeast Asia and that it was consumed as far back as 221 B.C., during the Tsin dynasty. (Then again, that book was written by the same fellow who wrote *Urine: The Holy Water* .)

If the online histories of *kombucha* are to be believed, SCOBYs made their way from China to Russia and Europe, and then to the rest of the world. In his 1968 book, *Cancer Ward,* Aleksandr Solzhenitsyn described a brew called *chaga,* made from a "birch-tree cancer . . . a sort of ugly growth on old birch trees . . . It is dome-shaped, black on the outside and dark brown inside." According to Solzhenitsyn, the people who drank *chaga* (because they were too poor to afford real tea) were free of cancer. The birch-tree "cancer" might have been a SCOBY, which has been found on plants that have sweet-tasting sap.

It's difficult to separate fact from fiction when it comes to *kombucha.* I've read that it prolongs life, prevents cancer, stops insomnia, reverses baldness, turns gray hair dark, is an excellent aphrodisiac, cures arthritis, and effectively treats dozens of other maladies. There are no studies to back up such extravagant claims, however.

Nevertheless, some of the research points to possible health benefits. An article published in 2009 in *Chinese Medicine* reports that *kombucha* was demonstrated to repair cellular damage in rats exposed to the industrial toxin trichloroethylene (TCE). Most of the health claims for *kombucha* come from the fact that it contains beneficial bacteria, also known as probiotics, such as *Lactobacillus* and *Saccharomyces boulardii.*

In one study in Sweden in 2005, researchers gave ninety-four workers in one company a daily dose of *Lactobacillus reuteri* for eighty days. They gave eighty-seven other workers a placebo. The results were impressive: The placebo takers called in sick more than twice as often as the bacteria takers, and the placebo takers' sick leaves lasted more than twice as long. Among the fifty-three shift workers (as opposed to day workers), "33% in the placebo group reported sick during the study period as compared with none in the *L. reuteri* group." Other tests have revealed that probiotic drinks could fight some kinds of cancers.

I also came across a few sobering items about *kombucha*. A book called *Medical Toxicology* reports that while consuming four ounces of *kombucha* a day "may not cause adverse effects in healthy people," people who drink excessive quantities or who have health problems could be putting themselves at risk. One person who applied *kombucha* to the skin for pain relief contracted cutaneous anthrax. Two *kombucha* drinkers ended up with "severe lactic acidosis"; one died. And one case of hepatitis was "associated with use of the tea." The book states that commercial preparations of *kombucha* evaluated by the FDA were found to be free of "pathogenic organisms" but that homebrewed *kombucha* is subject to all kinds of dangerous microscopic beasties.

After weighing the risks and benefits of *kombucha*, I decided to side with Sandor Ellix Katz, author of *Wild Fermentation: The Flavor, Nutrition, and Craft of Live-Culture Foods*. In his book, which is part how-to guide and part manifesto for taking back ownership of one's food, Katz writes:

> *There is a mystique surrounding fermented foods that many people find intimidating. Since the uniformity of factory fermentation products depends upon thorough chemical sterilization, exacting temperature controls, and controlled cultures, it is widely assumed that fermentation processes require these things. The beer- and winemaking literature tends to reinforce this misconception.*
>
> *My advice is to reject the cult of expertise. Do not be afraid. Do not allow yourself to be intimidated. Remember that all fermentation processes predate the technology that has made it possible for them to be made more complicated. Fermentation does not require specialized equipment. Not even a thermometer is necessary (though it can help). Fermentation is easy and exciting. Anyone can do it. Microorganisms are flexible and adaptable. Certainly there is considerable nuance to be learned about any of the fermentation processes, and if you stick*

*with them, they will teach you. But the basic processes are simple and straightforward. You can do it yourself.*

Katz's book (which was recommended to me by Kelly Coyne and Erik Knutzen of the Homegrown Evolution blog) not only has a recipe for making *kombucha* (he mentions that his friend likes to brew it using Mountain Dew instead of sweetened tea). It also has recipes for yogurt, sauerkraut, mead, miso, kimchi, tempeh, pickles, cheeses, sour cream, sourdough bread, wines, and many other bacteria-rich foods.

Katz, who calls himself a "fermentation fetishist," lives in the Short Mountain Sanctuary, "a queer intentional community" in rural Tennessee. He has AIDS and believes that fermented foods are an important part of keeping himself healthy. But the most important aspect of fermented foods for Katz is that its techniques are "ancient rituals that humans have been performing for many generations. They make me feel connected to the magic of the natural world, and to our ancestors, whose clever observations enable us to enjoy the benefits of these transformations." He also believes fermentation is a way to counteract the effects of industrially processed food that's consumed by people who have been "completely cut off from the process of growing food, and even from the raw products of agriculture." I found his ideas on fermentation to be inspiring and applicable to other DIY endeavors.

I decided to start making *kombucha* again and to try some of Katz's other recipes, too. Since I didn't know anyone with a SCOBY they could share with me, I sent $25 via PayPal to a Web site that sells a little plastic test tube filled with a bit of SCOBY floating in liquid. I added it to a gallon of tea-steeped sugar water, and in a couple of weeks, a large SCOBY was covering the tea. (I since learned that I could have just bought a bottle of *kombucha* for a few bucks from the market and used that as a starter.) Jane, my younger daughter, enjoys helping me prepare a batch of *kombucha,* though she can't stand the taste (which is just as well, as I only want consenting adults who've been apprised of the risks to be drinking it anyway). Carla likes the taste as much as I do, especially since I discovered that it comes out fizzier, more tart, and less sweet when it's been brewing for a month, which Katz and others recommend, not just a week, as I'd been doing back in 1995. Together, Carla and I go through a gallon in about three days. That means that, to supply our needs, I keep nine gallons brewing in the pantry closet and one gallon in the refrigerator for drinking. When we finish the batch in the refrigerator, I grab the oldest one from the closet and start a new batch. Making *kombucha* has become a twice-weekly part of our lives.

With my *kombucha* routine in full swing, I turned my efforts to yogurt and sauerkraut. Our family now goes through a gallon of kraut and more than five gallons of yogurt every month. Hardly a day goes by that I'm not in the kitchen making a batch of one of these three foods, which I never get tired of eating. All three are incredibly simple to make, and the ingredients are very cheap compared to what we'd pay for the finished products in a supermarket.

It costs me fifty cents to make a gallon of *kombucha*; in the store, a pint bottle costs $3, which means a gallon costs $24. I make sixteen eight-ounce jars of yogurt a week, which costs $6 total; the supermarket charges at least $16 for the same number of eight-ounce containers. Sauerkraut requires nothing more than noniodized salt (iodine prevents fermentation) and cabbage, which I buy for $1 a head at the farmers' market. Three heads make a gallon, so my sauerkraut costs seventy-five cents a quart. If you buy nonpasteurized sauerkraut at a supermarket, you'll pay about $6 a quart, and even then it will have been cooked at a temperature of about 140 degrees to kill off most of the bacteria (otherwise the sauerkraut juice could seep through the seal between the jar and the lid).

But even if I wasn't saving money, I'd still make these foods myself. That way, I am able to adjust the flavors to suit our tastes by adjusting the fermentation time or tweaking the ingredients. And, most important, I enjoy doing it.

My success with *kombucha,* yogurt, and sauerkraut has emboldened me to try more of the recipes in *Wild Fermentation.* Miso is next on my list. To make it, I need to get some *koji,* rice that has *Aspergillus oryzae* spores growing on the grains. It takes a year or more for the *koji* and soybeans to turn into miso, but I've learned that slowing down is part of the joy of being a DIYer. I'm willing to wait.

# 8 | KEEPING BEES

"I have established mystic contact with the spiritual core of apiculture, and now anything is possible."

—CHARLES MARTIN SIMON, ORIGINATOR OF
BACKWARDS BEEKEEPING

In 2008 I noticed that fewer bees were buzzing around my yard. Later, I found my fruit tree harvest to be much smaller than in previous years. The problem doesn't just exist in my backyard. There's a massive bee die-off going on all over the United States, and while speculation abounds (is it mites? microbial pathogens? pesticides? genetically modified crops? air pollution? pathogens? cell phone radiation?), no one really knows for certain the causes of what has been called "colony collapse disorder," or CCD. It's likely that CCD is caused by a number of these factors. In September 2009 a *New York Times* blog ran an article in which several bee experts offered their ideas on the subject. One, Rowan Jacobsen, author of *Fruitless Fall: The Collapse of the Honey Bee and the Coming Agricultural Crisis,* concluded, "It looks like the pieces of the colony collapse disorder puzzle are starting to fit together. And we can stop arguing about who was right: The virus camp, the fungus camp, the pesticide camp, the varroa mite camp, or the nutrition camp. It turns out everybody was right. (Well, everybody except the cell-phone and microwave-tower camps.)"

CCD is a big deal to beekeepers, since the big money in bee-keeping isn't honey but in mobile pollination services. Every February, bees are transported to the Central Valley in California to pollinate blossoms on a half-million acres of almond trees. If almond growers depended on natural pollinators like wild insects and bats, they could expect about 40 pounds of almonds per acre; with colonies of bees for hire, they can increase the yield to a whopping 2,400 pounds per acre. When almond blossom season is over, the mobile beekeepers, some of whom own tens of thousands of hives, load the hives onto semi trailers and ship them to other parts of California to pollinate other crops. In the summer, the beekeepers truck the bees north, where they make honey from alfalfa and clover nectar.

The pollination business has been hit hard by colony collapse disorder. There were 5 million managed bee colonies in 1940; today there are 2.5 million.

I decided to start keeping bees, both to pollinate my trees and vegetable garden and to provide wax and honey. It would be useful and fun, I thought, and I'd be doing my part to reverse the losses of CCD.

When I told my friend Kevin Kelly, a writer and beekeeper in Pacifica, California, he smiled in approval. He knew I was already raising chickens.

"You can read everything that's interesting about chickens in one night," Kevin warned. "But you can read about bees every night for the rest of your life."

One reason bees are so interesting is that, like people, bees are social animals that lead structured, complex, and orderly lives. Another reason is that bees are mysterious creatures, performing their alchemical magic in the darkness of their hives. I'd never given a lot of thought to how bees actually made honey. I figured it involved nectar, but beyond that, I had no idea how they did it. One night over dinner, I polled everyone in the family. I guessed that bees stuffed pollen and nectar into the cells of their hives and then squirted some kind of glandular secretion into the cells, kicking off a reaction to convert it into honey. Here's what the others said:

Sarina: "They take it out of the combs."

Jane: "The bees break the pollen. Honey is inside."

Carla: "They breathe in pollen and mix it with some chemicals in their body to make honey."

We were all wrong. Our ideas about how bees make honey reminded me of children's drawings that depict carrots growing in farmers' fields orange-end up.

Honey comes from nectar, not pollen. Nectar, which is mainly sucrose and water, is produced by plants as an incentive for bees to pollinate. Field bees use long, tubular tongues to suck the nectar out of flowers, clovers, dandelions, and tree blossoms. It is stored in a second stomach, which can hold about seventy milligrams, or 150 flowers' worth, of nectar. That's quite a load for a bee to carry, since a bee weighs about that much itself.

Once a field bee gets back to the hive with a full tank, it offers the nectar to a house bee, which sucks the nectar out of the field bee's mouth and then chews it, all the while mixing it with an enzyme called invertase, which breaks down the nectar's sucrose into glucose and fructose. The house bee also adds another enzyme, called glucose oxidase, which goes to work on some of the glucose, turning it into gluconic acid and hydrogen peroxide, both of which make the honey resistant to microbial and fungal contamination. After half an hour of mixing, the house bee deposits the liquid into a cell of the honeycomb, and other worker bees fan their wings to cause some of the water to evaporate. When the liquid becomes viscous enough, they cap off the open cell with wax, and there the freshly made honey stays until the bees get hungry. A bee colony, which can consist of as many as eighty thousand bees, might eat two hundred pounds of honey each year.

I started reading up on beekeeping. The books all warned not to capture and use wild bees, because they were germ-laden and nasty-tempered and wouldn't produce nearly as much honey as commercial honeybees. But in early January 2009, before I placed my order for bees-by-mail, Eric Thomason from Ramshackle Solid told me that he'd joined a club called the Backwards Beekeepers. He invited me to come along to the next meeting.

## "WHO WANTS TO FIGHT AFTER A TURKEY DINNER?"

On a sunny Sunday morning, I drove up a ridiculously narrow street in Silver Lake, arriving at a house perched on the side of a hill. Eric was just arriving in his pickup. Together, we walked through the gate, past a swimming pool, and into a backyard overlooking the HOLLYWOOD sign and the Griffith Observatory.

A German shepherd barked crazily as we arrived but quickly calmed down. (For the rest of the morning the dog, Tiger, nuzzled his wet nose into my trouser legs and pushed his snout under my arm in an attempt to get me to pet him.) A few people were sitting on lawn furniture. Eric and I shook hands with the homeowner—an architect named Leonardo—and a couple of other club members. The founder of the club, Kirk, was there, too. He wore a Birkenstock gimme cap, a green T-shirt, and old blue jeans hoisted up with suspenders. With his wire-frame glasses and gray walrus mustache, he looked like a younger Wilford Brimley.

As more members trickled in, I sat on a fraying wicker chair and listened to Kirk talk about bees. He has a rough but pleasant down-home accent and a colorful way with words that makes everything he says a delight to listen to. One of the club members asked him about the best place to order bees from.

"Don't buy 'em," he said. "The bees you buy commercially are sick; they're fucked up because they feed 'em chemicals and corn syrup and all kinds of shit. It's just like tenting a house for termites with you being stuck inside the house."

This was surprising to me. "I read that wild bees were too mean to use," I said.

"If you've got mean bees," Kirk said, "you get rid of the queen. The bees will make a new queen." (The queen is the only female bee in a colony that is able to reproduce.) He also warned me against buying queens by mail. Before shipping, queen bees are anesthetized with carbon monoxide gas, their wings are clipped, and they're artificially inseminated, a process that's contrary to the let-bees-be-bees philosophy of backwards beekeeping.

Another newbie pointed to Kirk's bee smoker, which looked like a little teakettle hooked up to an accordion, and asked him why beekeepers pumped smoke on bees when they were opening the hive boxes.

"The smoke makes them eat honey," he said. They assume their home is on fire, and so they gorge on honey to store up energy in case they have to escape. It has the desirable side effect of making them drowsy. "It's like you eating a bunch of turkey. Who wants to fight after a turkey dinner?"

Kirk quickly caught on that a number of us at this meeting knew next to nothing about bees, and what little we did know was in complete opposition to the tenets of Backwards Beekeeping. "We're totally ass-backwards to everyone else," Kirk explained. "That's why it works. Bees are the interface Mother Nature put in to make life work. The reason bees are the way they are is because that's what works." The idea of backwards beekeeping is to do as little as possible to interfere with the natural behavior of bees, and, as Kirk says, "just smile at 'em when you come out and see 'em."

The late Charles Martin Simon originated the backwards-beekeeping philosophy. In 2001 Simon, owner of a stinging-insect removal business in Santa Cruz, California, with more than four decades of beekeeping experience, issued his tenth "Principles of Beekeeping Backwards," a manifesto for people who wanted to try a more natural style of beekeeping:

> *Our apicultural forefathers, those great men who defined the principles of modern beekeeping, Langstroth, Dadants, Root . . . why were they so extravagantly successful? The answer is simple: because they didn't know what they were doing. They made it up, as it were, as they went along. That is the creative principle, and that is the way it works. Once the standards have been set and carved in stone, the pictures and diagrams and procedures etched into the books, we have then models to live up to, and we can't do it. Everything that comes after primary is secondary, or less. It will never be the same. For us to succeed, we have to become primary. We have to view beekeeping with entirely new eyes, just as our great pioneers did.*

This reminded me of what Sandor Ellix Katz wrote in his book *Wild Fermentation,* waving aside beer- and winemaking books that instruct the amateur brewer or winemaker to follow rigorous rules about "chemical sterilization, exacting temperature controls, and controlled cultures." (See chapter 7 for more on Katz's advice to "reject the cult of expertise.")

As Charles Martin Simon once did, Kirk earns a living removing wild bee colonies that have infested fences, trees, and chimneys. But instead of killing the bees, as many pest-control companies do,

Kirk saves the bees and resells them to people like me who want to keep them.

Kirk's been keeping bees since 1970, when he ordered a hive through Montgomery Ward. Someone asked him if it was legal to keep bees in Los Angeles. He replied, "I don't know what the laws are, but it could be you aren't supposed to have them." (I've since learned that urban beekeepers don't want to know the regulations for beekeeping for fear of finding out that they are violating one ordinance or another. I'm following suit.)

Another person asked Kirk about mites, the bane of the modern beekeeper. Mites (members of the Acarina order like another well-loved eight-legged creature, the tick) are pinhead-sized parasites that make a living by attaching their jaws to larger animals and drinking their blood. Several kinds of mites are parasitic on bees. The most infamous is the rust-colored varroa mite, which attaches itself to adult bees as well as to larvae and pupae. As many as a dozen mites at a time will latch onto one bee.

And the problem seems to be getting worse. According to researchers at Ohio State University, bee mites have "all but decimated the casual beekeeper and feral (wild) bees in North America."

Mites can wreak havoc on a colony by weakening the immune system of adult bees and by spreading a virus that causes wing deformities in undeveloped bees. The mites also hamper the ability of worker bees to make glucose oxidase, the enzyme that preserves honey. Without the enzyme, the honey becomes contaminated with bacteria, which poisons the bees. A mite infestation can lay waste to an otherwise healthy bee colony in a couple of weeks.

Varroa mites (the scientific name is *Varroa destructor*) have become a worldwide problem. Thought to have originated in Russia, they spread through Europe and were first discovered infesting

U.S. bees in 1987 in Wisconsin and Florida. A year later, the mites had spread to ten other states.

As you might expect, the first line of defense against bee mites has been chemical pesticides. And, as you might expect, after a couple of years of good results, mites have evolved to resist these chemicals.

"Bees have to live with mites, because they are in the environment," Kirk told us. Mites of all kinds are everywhere, and we'll never get rid of them. Tiny (and harmless) face mites are living in the hair follicles in your facial skin right now as you read this, eating sebaceous secretions and dead skin cells.

Instead of poisoning mites, the backwards way of controlling the parasites is to make patties out of vegetable shortening and sugar and feed them to the bees. The grease gets on their bodies, making it hard for mites to recognize the bees as suitable hosts.

After we watched a video of Kirk dismantling a fence to get at a wild-bee colony whose long, droopy hives looked like gray gym socks filled with sand, he passed around a pad of paper. "Everyone who wants bees, write down your e-mail and phone number. We'll call you soon and give you some bees."

A couple of days later, he sent an e-mail to everyone in the club that read:

> OK Beekeepers.
>
> To all club members with bees. Spring is starting to really go now. Your bees are probably bringing in pollen and making honey. Just check them once a week and make sure they have room to expand. If you have any questions call me. Now, all the new Beekeepers who are on the list for bees, make sure you've got your equipment ready. The swarms, and calls for bee removal, will be picking up

soon. Be ready. For the new guys with any questions about starter strips you can call me. I also posted some pictures here on the club page. Kirk

I wasn't ready. I had no equipment, so I needed to get it fast. Thankfully, Amy Seidenwurm, who founded the club along with Kirk and her husband, Russell Bates, posted a list of equipment to buy:

**FOR THE HIVE:**
*Top board*
*Bottom board*
*2 hive boxes (medium boxes are easier to move around than large ones)*
*20 frames (make sure they are the size to fit the boxes)*
*Hive tool*
*The cheapest smoker you can find (they all work the same)*

**YOUR GEAR:**
*Some kind of veil/hat getup*
*Gloves*

**YOU MAY ALSO WANT:**
Beekeeping for Dummies *book*
*A magnifying glass to see eggs*

So on a Saturday in late January 2009, I put Jane in the car, and we drove to Los Angeles Honey, the only beekeeping-supply store in the city. After taking an exit off the San Bernardino Freeway, I drove through a gritty industrial neighborhood of used auto parts warehouses, scrapyards, and metal recycling centers. In the gloomy drizzle the neighborhood looked like a scene out of a post-apocalyptic science fiction movie. I saw a group of men on the side of the road with a pickup piled high with old TV sets, barbecue grills, and other cast-off detritus of the consumer age. One of them was handling a thick wad of cash, peeling off a few bills to purchase some items from a man who had a shopping cart loaded with stuff he'd probably scavenged from Dumpsters.

So *this* is where all the stuff bought at Walmart that people no longer want ends up: It gets resold as scrap to street dealers and recycled into new raw materials, which are probably shipped back to China to be melted and repoured into shiny new toys packed in Styrofoam and sold back to us.

I found Los Angeles Honey across the street from a muddy lot filled with teetering towers of old wooden pallets that men on forklifts were moving from place to place. I thought of Bertrand Russell's definition of work in his 1932 essay "In Praise of Idleness": "Work is of two kinds: first, altering the position of matter at or near the earth's surface relatively to other such matter; second, telling other people to do so. The first kind is unpleasant and ill paid; the second is pleasant and highly paid."

DIY is mostly work of the first kind, but people find it to be pleasant. The guys moving the pallets probably don't like their job, because they are being told to do it, rather than being self-directed. I liked putting together the components for my self-watering garden containers, but it was *my* idea to do it. If I had a job where I had to go all over town assembling garden containers because my boss told me to, I'm sure I'd start to loathe it.

I parked in front of the beekeeping store, and Jane and I entered the small lobby area. We were the only customers, and I couldn't see anyone behind the counter separating the lobby from the cavernous warehouse in the back. It was clean and well-lighted inside, a startling contrast to the grimy, haphazard, industrial hubbub outside. The warehouse had metal shelves stacked fastidiously with wooden beehive materials.

Eventually a man appeared from behind one of the shelves at the far end of the warehouse. His orange-and-black-checked shirt, round belly, large-framed eyeglasses, thinning hair, and business-like demeanor gave him a distinctly beelike effect. I handed him my list of supplies. As he began collecting them from the shelves, I asked him a few questions.

His name was Larry, and his father had started the business in 1957, when Los Angeles still had a lot of fruit orchards and people on the periphery of the city still had large enough lots to keep bees without alarming their neighbors. When lots were subdivided and people started living in condos and apartments, the demand for hives plummeted. That's why, he said, one beekeeping-supply store really is sufficient for all of Los Angeles.

But Larry explained that in the last year business had increased. He figured it was because people wanted to pitch in to increase bee populations devastated by colony collapse disorder, and because they were tired of sitting in front of a computer all day long and wanted to spend more time outside. I told him that he was describing me, and he finally cracked a slight grin. "When you spend a lot of time with bees," he said, "you get to understand them. And that helps you begin to understand people."

He stacked my hive boxes (called supers) and other supplies on the countertop. "You have to attach the bottom cover to the bottom super," he said.

"How do I do that?" I asked him. Without answering, he went to the back, returning with four nails. He showed me where to put the nails, then handed them to me. I dropped the nails into the smoker so I wouldn't lose them. I also bought a beekeeper's outfit. I wanted to get one for Jane, too, but they didn't carry child sizes (I didn't bother asking for outfits that would fit Carla or Sarina as they'd already told me they didn't want to get close to the bees). I carried everything to my car, taking two trips to do so, then strapped Jane into her booster seat and drove home with my supplies.

# DOMESTIC HARMONY COLLAPSE DISORDER

Sometimes things just work out. Getting bees for my hive was one of them.

When we moved from Tarzana to Studio City in the spring of 2009, I noticed that lots of bees were buzzing around the roof of our new home. On closer inspection, it became clear that they were flying in and out of a crack in the outer wall of the second floor. They'd set up a colony between the walls.

When I told my friend Mark, a contractor whom we'd hired to do some remodeling, he told me he'd just finished a job in another part of town that had bees in the walls. They had hired an exterminator. When the poison gas was pumped into a hole in the wall, the thousands of bees in the colony had flapped their wings so vigorously that "it sounded like a 747," he recalled. "I could feel the wind from ten feet away." He said he felt sad for three days afterward.

Fortunately, Kirk ran a humane bee-removal service. I e-mailed him in early March 2009, telling him about the infestation and that the housepainter we'd hired didn't want to start painting until the bees were gone.

Kirk replied:

> If they are in the wall, you have to dismantle that part of the house to cut them out. If they are trapped, it takes about six weeks to get them all out.

I shot back:

I'm willing to cut a hole in the exterior, but my wife won't let me wait six weeks for them to come out. What should I do?

Kirk:

Well, to get them out, you have to remove the siding or whatever the outside is made of. If stucco or wood siding—very expensive, time intensive. Plus they are up high. Have you thought of a painter who isn't afraid of bees? If you want, have the painter deduct what it would cost to paint that part, and I will trap out the bees and then paint that part, or you have to kill them, I guess.

I really didn't want to kill the bees. Sean, our housepainter, was a compassionate soul, so he wrapped himself in a makeshift bee-protection suit consisting of a dust mask, duct tape, and overalls. He painted the bee-infested area without getting stung. Now we didn't have to rush, and Kirk could set up the bee trap without having to partially dismantle the house.

Kirk arrived on a Friday in late March in his pickup truck. He donned his beekeeper's suit, indelibly stained from years of contact with propolis, the plant-based resin bees use as a glue for maintaining their colonies. Then he climbed a ladder, caulking gun in hand, and patched up the crack the bees were using to fly in and out of the wall space. He sealed up the crack completely, except for a small hole. He plugged this hole with a matchbox-sized gizmo called a bee escape, which allows bees to travel in one direction (in this case, out of the house) but not the other direction (back inside).

Kirk climbed down and pulled from his truck a white cardboard box about eighteen inches long and twelve inches wide and tall. It contained a "nuc" (pronounced "nuke," short for *nucleus*), which is a starter hive containing eggs, pollen, worker bees, and a queen. It had come from a colony Kirk had removed the day before in Redondo Beach. He carried the nuc up the ladder and secured it next to the bee escape. The plan was that the bees in the wall would come out via the bee escape, then collect nectar, pollen, water, or whatever their assignment happened to be. When they tried to go back into the wall, the bee escape would stop them. They'd fly around in circles looking for an opening and would eventually enter the opening in the nuc box. Once inside, they'd discover the queen and switch allegiance to her.

Kirk said he'd return in about a week and a half to remove the nuc.

The day before he was scheduled to arrive, I told Carla that my hive was ready to be installed. Carla, who doesn't like bugs of any kind, told me that she didn't want the bees coming anywhere near the house, and especially not near the swimming pool.

I argued that even if we didn't have a hive, the canyon below us would be full of bees and that they'd be buzzing around our house all summer anyway.

"But we'll have more because of the hive," she said. "How many bees are going to be in the hive, forty or fifty?"

"Forty or fifty?" I said. "Are you kidding? No, more like ten thousand."

"What!? We can't have that many bees on our property! We'll have swarms!"

"No, we won't," I assured her. "We already have that colony on the roof, and they don't bug us."

"That's because they're up so high that they won't come down to bother us."

"But they need to come down to get nectar from the flowers and blossoms," I said.

"Oh, great. When are they going to do that?" she said.

"Well, my point is that if they aren't bugging us now, when they're moved to a hive, away from the house, they won't bug us, either."

"How do you know? How far away do they need to be? Have you researched it?" she said.

I had to admit that I hadn't.

"I don't want bees to ruin our summer by the pool! None of your friends' wives would let them have bees."

"Please, just let me try," I said. "If they cause a problem, I'll get rid of them."

"I want the hive to be put in a place where there isn't a problem to begin with."

"OK. When Kirk comes tomorrow to take the bees out of the trap, you can talk to him about where we should put the hive," I said.

Carla reluctantly agreed. We had established a truce—albeit an uneasy one—in the beehive war.

The next day, as I was walking back to the house after tending to the chickens a little after 9 a.m., I saw Kirk pulling up in the driveway.

"Howdy!" he said, getting out of the truck.

"Hi, Kirk. Did we say 10 a.m.?"

"I'm usually early," he said. "Do you have your hive set up where you want it?"

"Not yet," I said. "I wanted to ask you about that. My wife is concerned that the bees will pester her and the kids if the hive is too close. She'll be here at ten or so."

"Well, then, let's put the hive as far from the house as we can," he said.

I led him to the backyard, to the same area where I was keeping the chickens. "My idea," I told him, "is to put the hive behind this bush, so if the bees fly toward our house, they'll have to fly up and over the bush, keeping them up over everyone's heads."

"OK," Kirk said.

"Will that work?" I asked.

"It might."

I used a shovel to make a level spot in the sloped dirt, then laid a couple of pieces of lumber down as a platform for the hive. Kirk and I set the super box down, then walked back to the front of the house to get the nuc, hopefully full of the bees from our house walls.

Kirk put on his beekeeping suit and told me to put mine on, too. As he was preparing to get the nuc box off the roof, I went in the house to put on my suit for the first time since trying it on for size at the store a couple of months earlier. When I came back out, Kirk was halfway up the ladder, holding a smoker in one hand. He lifted the lid to the nuc box and squeezed some smoke into it.

"Yep," he said, "there's brood in there." That meant that the bees were taking care of the new queen, so she could lay eggs. He replaced the lid.

I held on to the ladder to keep it steady as he climbed down with the nuc box tucked under one arm. He handed it to me. The box was buzzing like a vibrating cell phone. A couple of dozen bees were frantically orbiting around my head and body. My senses were on high alert. I knew the bee suit would protect me, but my lizard brain was telling me to drop the box and run.

It took a couple of minutes to carry the nuc box to the hive, and it was difficult to walk on the steep slope carrying a box of bees while wearing the beekeeper's mask. At last, we reached the hive.

"Now, lift off the top," Kirk said. I thought he meant the top of the nuc box. When I took it off, a bunch of agitated bees shot out, circling wildly.

Kirk stayed calm.

"Put the lid back on. Take the top off the *hive,* and use your hive tool"—it looks something like a small crowbar—"to remove five frames."

I didn't have my hive tool with me, so I had to go back into the house to get it. When I returned, I used it to lift out the frames. Kirk instructed me to lift the top of the nuc box, and he gave the bees a squirt of smoke, which immediately knocked them into a daze. The nuc box had five frames in it. They had combs on them, and hundreds of bees were crawling around them. I lifted the frames out and placed them in the hive box one at a time. The stupefying effect of the smoke began to wear off, and the bees started moving more frantically. The pitch of the buzzing went higher. I hurried to get the rest of the frames in.

"When the bees get more active like that," Kirk said, "it's natural for you to want to move quickly. But it's the time for you to slow down. We're in no hurry." I followed his advice and finished transferring the frames at a normal pace. I put the lid on, and we walked back to the house to have a cup of tea and a snack.

We'd been sitting at the kitchen table for a few minutes when Carla arrived. It was about ten-thirty. She said hello and asked how things were going.

"We got the bees into the hive," I told her.

"Oh, really?" she said, her back turned to us, putting dishes into the dishwasher. Kirk didn't notice the hint of sharpness in her question but, being her husband, I instantly knew she wasn't happy that we'd already populated the hive without waiting for her to OK the location.

Kirk stayed around a little longer, setting up another nuc box on the roof to capture more bees—apparently, the colony living in the walls of our house was large. When he left, I went back into the kitchen, where Carla was cleaning up.

"Is everything OK?" I asked hopefully.

Carla turned. "You were supposed to wait until I came back before you put the beehive down."

"I'm sorry," I said. "He got here early, but I talked to him about the best place to put the hive, and he said the spot I picked was a good one."

"Show me."

I led her outside, past the pool, past the chicken coop, to the bush at the far end of the yard.

"Oh, no!" she said. "They'll be flying all around the pool."

"No, they won't," I said.

"How do you know?" she said.

And then we had the same argument as before, only a little more loudly.


# BEES IN THE BELFRY

One evening not long after Kirk's visit, the family gathered upstairs to watch a movie. Sarina pointed out that the recessed lights in the ceiling weren't as bright as usual.

"I think there are bees in them," she said.

I was about to blurt out, "That's impossible," but lately so many things had been going wrong with our bees and chickens (the coyotes had started snacking on the hens at this point) that I kept my mouth shut and peered up at the glass light enclosures in the ceiling.

Sure enough, they were filled with dead bees. That meant that the colony that had taken up residence in our walls was also in the space between the roof and the ceiling. In fact, one of the glass cups was so packed with bees that they were blocking out the light from the bulb entirely. We called off the movie, and I sent every-one downstairs while I removed the glass cups and got rid of the bees (which were all dead, presumably from the heat of the bulbs). There were thousands of them all over the floor. I had to empty the Dustbuster a few times to get them all.

Carla made a gagging sound and turned her head in disgust when I brought down a glass cup full of dead bees.

"This is horrible," she said. "Our house is filled with bees. I thought you and Kirk had taken care of the problem."

"I thought we had, too," I said meekly. What else could I say? Between this and the chicken deaths, I was flunking animal husbandry. "I'll call Kirk and ask him what to do next."

"Are they going to make a hole in the wall and swarm through?" said Carla.

"No," I said. "They can't chew a hole through the wall." I sounded more confident than I felt—at this point, I felt like I didn't know anything about bees.

I e-mailed Kirk, and he said he'd come by to check things out. In the meantime, I'd been checking on the bees in the hive out back, and they didn't seem to be doing very well. The ones from the five honeycombed frames that Kirk and I had added to the hive seemed to be ignoring all of the other frames: They were devoid of comb. Once again, I e-mailed Kirk and asked him what was happening. He replied:

> Hey Mark, it has been a bad year for honey. Not much going on. You should maybe feed them. But let me come over and help set it up. It is ant season.

Ants are a natural enemy of bees.

Kirk said he'd come over and inspect my hive when the Backwards Beekeepers club met at my house. In late August, more than fifty people showed up for the meeting, and while Carla served snacks to everyone and I manned the espresso machine, Kirk donned his bee suit and went out to peek at my hive. He returned with bad news. The entire colony, or what had been left of it, had absconded. The hive was completely empty. Kirk wasn't exactly sure why the bees had left, but he thought I ought to try feeding my next batch of bees sugar water as a way of encouraging them to stick around.

"Meet me at the Solano Community Garden in Chinatown on Thursday, and we'll get you some more bees."

I was frustrated that my bees had left in search of better accommodations, especially on the heels of my chicken die-off. But I reminded myself that every chicken keeper I'd met had lost chickens to predators or illness, and that several other people in the bee club had lost their bees. Losing animals, as sad as it might be, is part of the homesteading experience. My job, I decided, was to get better at it to keep those losses to a minimum.

The following Thursday I drove to Chinatown and met Kirk at the garden, built on the grounds of an elementary school that was torn down in 1935. I parked my car, collected my bee suit out of the back, and entered through a gate. About thirty small garden plots were growing flowers and vegetables. I didn't see anyone else in the lot, but I smelled the odor of smoldering newspapers, which meant a bee smoker was in the vicinity.

I followed the smoke smell and found Kirk and two other members of the bee club dressed in their bee suits. I put mine on and helped them wrangle a half dozen or so hive boxes full of bees that Kirk had recently pulled from people's houses and fences. After transferring five frames to a cardboard box for one of the club members, Kirk told me it was my turn to prepare one of the boxes to take back to my house.

He pointed to a weather-beaten box and told me to take off the top. It was crammed with bees. Kirk squirted a little smoke on them, and they scurried into the depths of the box.

"They're busy eating honey now," Kirk said. I fetched a framed screen, and Kirk told me to use it to cover the top of the box and secure it with masking tape. I made sure the bees were sealed in, then taped the bottom to the box, too. The bees were now trapped inside. I carried the box—which didn't weigh nearly as much as I thought a box of fifteen thousand bees should weigh—through the gate and set it in the back of Kirk's pickup truck. Then we drove to my house in Studio City. Once there, I carried the bees to my hive and set them down. I gave Kirk one of the empty wooden boxes so he could use it on his next bee-removal call.

After we got the bees settled in, Kirk showed me how to make a simple spacer frame so that I could set a plastic bag filled with sugar water in the box and close the lid without squishing the bag. I thanked him for his help and paid him $75 for the bees.

Since they seemed to be agitated from the trip, I waited a day before disturbing them. Then, following Kirk's instructions, I filled a one-gallon Ziploc bag with a fifty-fifty sugar-water mixture and brought it out to the hive, along with a bee smoker. The smoker helped calm the bees, but they still tried to get at my face. I set the bag on top of the hanging frames and cut a two-inch slit so sugar water would seep out. Then I replaced the top.

While I was at the hive, I applied a stripe of sticky goop called Tanglefoot around the perimeter of the hive box. This was to keep the ants out. (Earlier I had swapped the top and bottom covers of the hive so that the bees had to enter and exit from the top of the box instead of the bottom, which is how hives are usually set up.) A number of the club members had been complaining that ants were decimating their hives, and Kirk said that the bees weren't able to stop ants because ants are too little to sting. While I was applying the Tanglefoot to the hive box, the smoke wore off, and the bees started going crazy. I remembered what Kirk had told me earlier about slowing down and taking it easy when bees were angry, so I kept my mind on the task at hand and tried to ignore the kamikaze bees. After I was done, I headed back to the house. The bees followed me about halfway and then gave up.

- - - - - - - - - -

So far, the bees seem to have adjusted to their new home, and they are consuming a couple of bags of sugar water each week. It bothers me a bit to think that I am feeding them sugar to keep them going, instead of having them get all their nourishment from nature, but Kirk assures me they will be able to find plenty of pollen and nectar when blossoms reappear.

I haven't fallen in love with beekeeping yet. For one thing, I have never been a fan of any activity requiring a suit—that's why I never went scuba diving again after getting my certification and why I don't like working in an office. Bee suits are hot and uncomfortable. And I don't feel emotionally attached to the bees the same way I do to my chickens. Bees are much more inscrutable than chickens; they have no personality. And frankly, they scare me a little. But I'm not giving up on my bees yet. The club members who have gone through a full year or more with their bees—who have harvested honey and seen how the bees pollinate their gardens and trees—are in love with the little creatures.

I hope that by this time next year I'll feel the same way.

# 9 LEARNING HOW TO LEARN

"Every one of us knows, if we stop to think about it, that the most valuable lessons we have learned are not what we 'learned in kindergarten,' nor what we learned in courses later on. They are, instead, the lessons that we learned when we allowed ourselves the luxury of following through on our own interests and our own drives to play, fully and deeply."

—PETER GRAY, "LEARNING REQUIRES FREEDOM"

Years ago, I read Ken Silverstein's bizarre and wonderful article in *Harper's* called "The Radioactive Boy Scout," about Eagle Scout David Hahn's attempt to build a nuclear breeder reactor (a machine that produces radioactive fuel faster than it consumes it) in his backyard garden shed. In 1994 the seventeen-year-old Hahn collected radioactive material for his breeder by driving around towns with a Geiger counter in the front seat. When the counter started clicking rapidly, he'd stop his car and enter the nearest store (usually an antiques or junk shop) and ask the proprietor to show him all the old clocks he had for sale.

Hahn was looking for clocks made prior to our understanding of the dangers of radioactivity, some of which had radium painted on the hands so they would glow in the dark. He would buy the radioactive clocks and then scrape the radium paint off for his experiment. He also collected radioactive materials from smoke detectors (they contain a speck of the synthetic element americium-241, which changes the electrical charge of smoke particles to make them trigger the alarm) and camping lantern mantles (some contain thorium to make them glow more brightly). One time Hahn hit the jackpot when he bought an old clock and found a small jar of radium paint in it, which was probably stored there to refresh the hands.

In the end, Hahn collected enough radioactive material in his mother's shed that a Geiger counter could detect it from five houses away. In 1995 an unrelated encounter with the local police resulted in the discovery of the goings-on in the garden shed. The find triggered a Federal Radiological Emergency Response. Both the FBI and the Nuclear Regulatory Commission were called in, and Hahn's mother's property was declared a Superfund cleanup site. The chemicals and other contaminated materials were placed in thirty-nine barrels and taken to a dump facility called Envirocare in the Great Salt Lake Desert, where other radioactive waste is kept.

Afterward, Hahn graduated from high school, attended community college, and served in the military. But his fascination with radioactive materials apparently had a long half-life: In 2007 he was arrested in Michigan for stealing sixteen hallway smoke detectors from the apartment building he lived in. His mugshot was truly frightening: His face was completely covered with red and black sores, which authorities thought to be radiation burns. He pleaded guilty and was sentenced to ninety days in jail.

Silverstein's article mentioned that Hahn had been inspired to practice chemistry after reading *The Golden Book of Chemistry Experiments*. Published in 1960, the book is long out of print. Since reading the article, I'd wanted to own a copy, but I didn't want to fork

over the $200 or more that used copies go for. One day, on a lark, I searched the BitTorrent sharing sites and found a PDF version. The experiments in the book include making chlorine, ammonia, hydrogen, and ethanol. I was astounded. In today's litigious environment, few publishers would dare publish a book like this for fear of getting sued—teaching kids how to make their own alcohol? Even if a publisher were willing to take the risk, the chemicals and lab equipment necessary to perform the experiments are not easy to obtain, not only because they are considered dangerous but because the Drug Enforcement Administration doesn't want anyone using them to make methamphetamines. Today's chemistry sets are all but useless, because they don't contain any chemicals that might be dangerous.

So if kids are no longer able to learn chemistry at home, at least they can learn it in school, right? Unfortunately, real chemistry labs are disappearing from schools. Robert Bruce Thompson is an amateur chemist and the author of *The Illustrated Guide to Home Chemistry Experiments* (published by *Make*). According to Thompson, No Child Left Behind is killing high school chemistry because schools are overly concerned with making sure students do well on standardized tests. "You can't really blame the teachers and administrators," he told a reviewer. "Their jobs depend on students scoring well in reading and math, so guess what they focus all their attention on teaching?"

If book publishers, chemistry set manufacturers, and schools aren't providing the materials and information needed to experience chemistry, does that mean young people (and curious adults) are out of luck?

Absolutely not. As Thompson has pointed out, amateurs have been practicing chemistry since long before the first chemistry set was made (around 1930 or so). His book features more than four hundred experiments, along with suggestions on how to obtain

the chemicals and lab gear needed to conduct them. (For example, chemicals that have been banned from chemistry sets are often available in the form of solvents or reagents that can be picked up at any well-stocked hardware store.)

Amateur chemistry is just one facet of the amateur-science movement, which has been around in one form or another since people started wondering about the way the universe and the things in it work. But it has been enjoying a renaissance recently, thanks to the idea-transceiving power of the Internet. A quick Google search will lead you to communities of microscope and telescope builders, instructions for making DNA-replicating equipment, guides to blowing your own chemistry glassware—thousands of science-based Web sites.

You might say the Internet saved amateur science from an ignominious death. A hundred and fifty years ago, the practice was thriving. *Popular Science* ran columns like "Adventures with Your Microscope" and "Home Laboratory Chemistry." They offered experiments to study luminescence and crystal formation, recreate famous bridges and other architectural structures out of toothpicks, make a tiny oil refinery, and superheat steam to a temperature high enough to light a cigarette. As late as April 1964 *Popular Science* was singing the praises of DIY science, running an article calling for ten million amateur scientists to advance the fields of astronomy, meteorology, and oceanography.

In 1928, *Scientific American* launched its "Amateur Scientist" column, which detailed such projects as constructing an electron accelerator, making amino acids, photographing air currents, measuring the metabolic rate of small animals, extracting antibiotics from soil, culturing aquatic insects, tracking satellites, constructing an atom smasher, extracting the growth substances from a cantaloupe, conducting maze experiments with cockroaches, making an electrocardiogram of a water flea, constructing a

Foucault pendulum, building a Geiger counter, and experimenting with geotropism. Who knew you could have so much fun at the kitchen table?

One might argue that building an apparatus to measure the speed of light is a wasted effort, since someone else figured that one out a long time ago. But to construct the device and take the measurements yourself is a deeply rewarding experience. There is a certain satisfaction in knowing for yourself the speed of light, or the size of the Earth, or the distance from the Earth to the Moon, or the acceleration of gravity. (This must have been what Ronald Reagan meant when he said, "Trust, but verify.")

As I browsed issues of *Popular Science* through the decades, I found that coverage of amateur science petered out in the 1960s, to be replaced almost exclusively by articles about Big Science, the kind that costs billions of dollars and requires an army of Ph.D.s to oversee. And even though *Scientific American* continued to run "Amateur Scientist" until 2000, its focus, too, shifted away from do-it-yourself science toward passive edutainment. Perhaps these magazines were forced to keep up with the shifting interests of their readers. In the 1970s many amateur scientists, and those who might have become ones, turned their attention to personal computers, shifting their hobby from the real to the virtual universe. And when the World Wide Web appeared in the early 1990s, the same types of smart and curious people flocked to it, eager to discover what could be done with this new and awesomely powerful form of mass media.

By 1980 the era of science-as-hobby was dead. And it stayed that way for a good long while. But in the last five years, amateur science has returned. It's as though the folks who have been spending all their time creating the Web and everything on it suddenly looked up from their monitors and realized that the world itself was the ultimate hackable platform. In other words, for these creative

DIY folks, the Internet stopped being an end in itself and became a tool to get things done in the real world. The early rush of creating the Web was over, and now the smart, creative geeks who built it were spending more time in the physical world.

The Internet inspires and accelerates amateur scientific research by making it possible to share reports, videos, blueprints, data, and discussions. Amateur scientists are using the Internet exactly as its architects first envisioned it forty years ago—as a scientific research facilitator, replacing snail mail, print-based peer-reviewed journals, and conferences. It has brought far-flung researchers together in a shared space where communication is instant and ideas flow at nearly the speed of light.

Who better to explain this new explosion in amateur science than Forrest M. Mims III? Mims is the editor of *The Citizen Scientist,* an online newsletter published by the Society for Amateur Scientists. The sixty-five-year-old Texan is known chiefly for two things: writing a series of extremely popular electronics hobby books for RadioShack in the 1980s and cofounding the company that developed the Altair 8800, widely regarded to be the first personal computer. Mims has no advanced degree in science but has written for peer-reviewed journals like *Nature* and is frequently hired as a consultant by the U.S. government and other institutions.

Mims's curiosity is wide-ranging; he conducts experiments in biology, geology, astronomy, botany, and meteorology. Nothing in the natural world escapes his interest. His recent articles and experiments have explored flint tool–making techniques, jellyfish, owls, moss that grows on trees, windmill technology, planetary meteor scarring, helium production, tree rings, the ozone layer, mosquito infestations, volcanoes, plant fibers, rat snakes, spear grass, and water vapor. The December 2008 issue of *Discover* magazine included him among the "50 best brains in science" (which caused a minor media furor, thanks to Mims's assertion that Darwinian evolution is hogwash and his stated doubts that $CO_2$ levels significantly affect global warming).

I e-mailed Mims and told him, by way of introduction, that I still owned the copy of his *Getting Started in Electronics* that I bought for $2.95 at RadioShack in 1985. I asked if he'd be willing to be interviewed, and he e-mailed me back immediately with his telephone number, telling me to call after he'd finished taking his daily backyard measurements of ultraviolet radiation and ozone levels with his homebuilt apparatus. I waited an hour or so and rang him up. After we exchanged pleasantries, Mims launched into an attack on the traditional education system as a destroyer of the DIY spirit.

"I probably would have been diagnosed with ADD as a kid," he said, "because I didn't pay attention. I was bored to death by conventional education. My mind was wandering all during class, inventing things or traveling to foreign countries or whatever. That didn't mean I was stupid. It meant I thought a little bit differently than my neighbor. If they'd put me on medication, maybe I'd be on welfare today. Who knows? We are totally dumbing down the country by not fully understanding these things."

Mims designed his first rocket guidance system while sitting in a seventh-grade English class at Hamilton Jr. High School in Houston. "I was looking at the fan on the wall and could see this idea for a new way of controlling a rocket in flight without using fins. That became a peer-review paper when I was an adult. I wasn't learning English—I didn't really care. All I cared about was inventing."

The year 1958 marked a turning point in Mims's life. He was at an amateur-rocketry meeting and saw a man using a small radio transmitter to remotely launch a rocket. He was stunned to learn that the man had made the radio controller at home. "The influence of a young person seeing what somebody else can do is incredibly important," Mims told me. "Seeing that little transmitter in that rocket—that's what really motivated me. I thought, 'If that guy can do it, I can do it!'"

In addition to rockets and radio-controlled launch systems, Mims started making simple analog computers that could multiply two numbers. By the time he was a senior in high school in 1962, he had designed and built a Russian-to-English translator out of a homebuilt analog computer and some primitive digital circuitry.

Mims went to college, but after struggling with his first-year course in algebra, he realized that a traditional science education wasn't going to work out. He switched majors to government, graduating in 1966 from Texas A&M University. While in school he continued to experiment with electronics, developing a device to help blind people sense obstacles in their path and beep if they were in danger of walking into them.

Even though he didn't have a degree in science, Mims never stopped tinkering. In 1969, while serving in the air force, he cofounded Micro Instrumentation and Telemetry Systems (MITS) in Albuquerque, New Mexico. MITS built model-rocket telemetry devices, such as light flashers and radio transmitters, but the small company started branching out into selling electronics kits through ads in *Popular Electronics*. One of their kits was the Opticom, a voice transmitter that used light beams instead of radio waves as a signal.

When the kit sales proved disappointing, Mims sold back his share of equity to the other partners and began writing for electronics-hobbyist and model-rocketry magazines. MITS would later go on to make and sell the Altair 8800 in 1975. Mims wasn't at MITS during this time, but he was hired to write the operating manual. (Fun fact: Bill Gates and Paul Allen moved to Albuquerque so they could write software for the Altair 8800, eventually founding Microsoft.)

Mims became a well-known writer in the hobbyist book and magazine trade. One day RadioShack editor Dave Gunzel got a look at one of Mims's hand-drawn laboratory notebooks and fell in love with the neat lettering and charming anthropomorphic drawings of electronic components. He asked Mims to write a series of how-to books in the same style. "He even suggested using a crayon," Mims said. "I said, 'You can't do a book with a crayon. It has to be a pen or a pencil.'" Gunzel conceded the point, and Mims went to work, drawing and lettering two pages a day and suffering terribly from writer's cramp.

The suffering paid off. The first printing of a hundred thousand copies of *Getting Started in Electronics* sold out immediately. (The book is still in print by a different publisher and has sold in the neighborhood of 1.3 million copies. All together, Mims's thirty RadioShack titles have sold more than 7 million copies.)

RadioShack's books might have met with great success, but that didn't stop the company from going the way of *Popular Science* and *Scientific American*. Founded in Boston in 1921 by Theodore and Milton Deutschmann, two brothers who wanted to cash in on the amateur-radio boom, RadioShack served the electronics-hobbyist market until the 2000s, when it shifted over to hawking cell-phone plans and other consumer electronics products. "RadioShack dropped all their books about five years ago," Mims said, "which is one of the biggest mistakes they ever made, because the hobby parts were already going down, and then sales of electronic parts really dropped after that because there were no books to support the parts."

Undaunted, Mims continued to conduct his own experiments and to explore new branches of science to feed his insatiable curiosity. He said he takes a hands-off approach to his three children's education but has two rules: "If you're gonna be in my family, you go to church on Sunday and you do a science fair project every year. Those are the two requirements of being in my family." His children followed the rules, but he admits the teenage years were a little tougher to deal with. After son Eric (who had built a seismometer that picked up vibrations from two underground nuclear tests in Nevada) and eldest daughter Vicki (who calculated the sun's rotation by tracking the movement of sunspots) had moved out, Mims called to ask them if he had been too strict about his science-project rule. He was wondering whether to stay the course with his youngest daughter, Sarah.

"Those children told me—this was the first time they opened up to me—'We learned more from doing the science projects you made us do than from anything we learned in high school,'" Mims said. "And Sarah *wanted* to do it. She gave up being a cheerleader, and she's very good-looking."

Like her father, Sarah is something of a celebrity in amateur-science circles—"She's the most famous [of my children], just put her name into Google," Mims advised me. Sarah won first place at the science fair two years in a row at the Texas Junior Academy of Science. And while still a teenager, she was the lead author of a NASA paper about detecting smoke and dust that had traveled through air currents from thousands of miles away to her home in Seguin, Texas. As an eleventh-grader in 2002, Sarah designed and built an air sampler, sent it aloft in a kite, and examined the samples it collected. She found smoke particles from fires started by farmers in South America burning mold-infected crops in a backfiring attempt to sterilize the land before replanting it. Sarah also found living mold spores from the fires. An article published by NASA stated that "this surprising discovery from a young, amateur scientist has the potential to change the prevailing wisdom on the benefits of burning diseased crops or timber."

"The agricultural people haven't yet seen the implications of it," Mims said. "But they will. Because the inertia is so great, they don't always realize the significance of a major new discovery. Her discovery explained transport of disease organisms from plants across the ocean."

- - - - - - - - -

Talking to Mims about his children's education (and self-education) made me think about the way my own children were learning. When Sarina, now a seventh-grader, was in second grade, she told Carla and me that math was "like a rainbow." I wasn't sure what she meant, but I figured it was good for her to associate math with something so pleasant. Her teacher told us she was one of her best students when it came to math.

For the next couple of years, Sarina continued to excel, but by the time she finished fifth grade, her standardized-test math score had dropped from the ninetieth percentile to the thirty-fifth. She was now telling us that she disliked math. We were concerned, not only because she had previously enjoyed the subject but because she would soon be attending middle school and we wanted to make sure she would be able to attend a good one. The standardized test she would take in the sixth grade, the ISEE, would be sent to all of the middle schools she'd be applying to.

Carla and I asked the parents of Sarina's classmates what they were planning to do about preparing their kids for the ISEE. Most said that they were signing their kids up for private tutoring sessions from an agency that specializes in the exam.

I didn't want Sarina to get tutoring for the test for three reasons. First, it cost $1,700 for ten lessons. Second, we would have to disclose the fact that she'd been tutored for the ISEE on her middle school applications. Third, and most important, I wanted to find out *why* Sarina was having difficulty with math, and I figured that the only way I could get to the bottom of it was by tutoring her myself.

When I told Carla that I wanted to teach Sarina math, she liked the idea. I was surprised, because Carla usually favors HAP (hire a pro) over DIY. I can't really blame her, not with my track record of starting ambitious projects and not finishing them, or else doing them badly and not going back to fix them. I insisted on installing tiles on the kitchen floor of our first house in Boulder, Colorado, shortly after we'd gotten married in 1988. I must have done something wrong with the grout, because many of the tiles cracked in the first few days. Every time we walked into the kitchen, the broken tiles served as a reminder of my incompetence and slothfulness. They were still cracked when we moved three years later. (I wonder if the current owners fixed them or not. I doubt it, because the last time I drove by the house, in 2005, the mailbox that had fallen off its mount when we lived there was still sitting on the porch steps where I'd set it down almost twenty years earlier.)

Another time, in 2003, Carla wanted to change the color of some doors in our house in Los Angeles from white to red. She wanted to call a painter, but I told her that I'd be able to handle a small job like that myself. I'd remembered seeing some red paint in our garage, left there by the people who had lived in the house before us. She agreed to let me do it, but not without reservation.

"Don't make it look bad," she warned.

"Of course I won't," I said, hurt at the insinuation that I could screw up such a simple task. I spread newspapers on the floor, found a brush, and began painting. It didn't take long to realize that something wasn't quite right with the paint. It was going on in streaks, thin and shiny. I had been hoping for more of a flat, even look. After I gave both doors a coat, the can was just about empty. I planned to buy more in the next day or two so I could apply another coat—and hopefully get rid of the streaky look— but I never made it to the paint store. Fortunately, guests assumed the streaky paint job was an intentional bit of flair and complimented us on the artistic touch, so Carla wasn't too upset. Even so, the lucky result did nothing to boost my reputation as a competent handyman.

With so many failed projects behind me, why did Carla so readily agree to let me tutor Sarina in math? After all, if I screwed up this project, the consequences might be far worse than cracked tiles. Our daughter's future was at stake. I couldn't risk letting that happen. And that's precisely why Carla let me do it. She knew that my sense of parental responsibility was too strong to let me slack off.

Deep down, I also hoped that my recent more-or-less successful DIY efforts had shown her that I was on my way to becoming a handyman of my word.

I ordered a copy of the ISEE preparation handbook, which contained sample tests, resolving that Sarina and I would work for one hour each week, on Sunday morning, for the twelve weeks until it was time for her to take the test. Sarina didn't complain about our plan—she wanted to get into a good school.

On the first Sunday, she and I went into the guesthouse and sat at my desk. I opened the book to the Quantitative Reasoning practice test, which had twelve questions. I told her I wanted her to take the practice test so we could find out which areas of math she needed to work on: algebra, fractions, decimals, percentages, or geometry.

"I'll just sit in this chair over here while you work," I said. "When you're done, we'll go over the answers together." I gave her several sharpened number-two pencils and a photocopy of the sheet used to mark her answers. I picked up a magazine and started reading.

After a couple of minutes of silence, Sarina sobbed, "I can't *do* this!" and threw her pencil on the desk. I jumped out of my chair and sat down next to her. She was stuck on the very first problem:

1. **Of the 500 people responding to a local survey, 238 answered "yes," 212 answered "no," and the rest were undecided. What percent of the people were undecided?**
   **Ⓐ** 47%     **Ⓑ** 42%
   **Ⓒ** 10%     **Ⓓ** 5%

I asked Sarina where she was getting stuck, and she wasn't able to tell me. She couldn't even get started. She was fighting back tears; this was a problem she felt she *should* know, because her class had been studying these types of word problems. As calmly as I could, I read the problem to her. Then I said, "After you read the question, you need to ask yourself what the missing information is, what the given information is, and how you can figure out the missing information from the given information. OK, what is the missing information?"

She didn't have an answer. I couldn't believe that her school hadn't prepared her for answering a question like this. But I kept my anger in check and led her along with questions and suggestions, letting her try, haltingly and with little real comprehension, to go through the steps needed to solve the problem.

I knew it would be pointless to have her take the rest of the test on her own, so I stayed at her side and we worked on the next three questions together. It took an hour. She had a great deal of trouble with each question, and there were points where she'd get panicky. I was able to calm her down every time she got emotional. I'm not sure how much she learned about math in that first lesson, but I was sure she now had a better idea of how to approach a test question.

Later that day, when I thought about the time we'd spent together, I realized how much I had enjoyed it. It was not at all boring to tutor her; in fact, it was tremendously interesting. I liked the challenge of teaching my child. What could be more natural than that? It felt right. Forrest Mims was onto something, mentoring his kids with science-fair projects. For most of Sarina's life, we'd farmed out the job of educating her. I'd never paid much attention to what she was learning, because I believed that paying someone else to take care of her education meant I didn't have to worry about it. Not only was I wrong; I was also missing out on a rewarding way to spend time with my daughter.

We increased our tutoring sessions to twenty minutes daily. Working together on problems, we connected on a deep level. I enjoyed helping her develop her math skills, and she enjoyed showing me that she was learning. As the days went by I could see her gaining confidence. Sarina was able to distill the essence of the problems and come up with methodical ways to solve them. She was making real progress.

It struck me that the last six years had been a missed opportunity. I could have been helping to teach Sarina for all these years, but I'd avoided it because I didn't think it would be interesting or useful. I started teaching math to my five-year-old, Jane, who had just entered kindergarten. Instead of telling her a bedtime story, I started giving her math problems. ("If you have six cherries and you want to share them with two of your friends so you all have the same number of cherries, how many cherries should you give to each friend?") She loved these questions, and ever since I started, she has asked for math problems every night and even in the day. I also bought a bunch of little plastic cubes to teach the powers of ten and percentages, and she has gotten a good grasp of both concepts.

- - - - - - - - -

Tutoring my daughters reminded me of an e-mail exchange I had a number of years ago with my friend Andrew Anker. I met Andrew in 1993 when he came to work at *Wired,* where I was an editor. He wrote the business plan for *HotWired,* the magazine's Web site, and became its CEO when it launched in April 1994. Andrew was a few years younger than me, with a sleepy expression, a couple of days' beard growth, and a permanent case of bed head. Despite his appearance, he talked quickly and energetically, and once he got going on a subject, his face would light up. I was impressed by his intelligence and knowledge of the Web, which was barely in its infancy in 1993. Andrew was on top of every new development that came along and knew how to incorporate the good ones into *HotWired* in a way that felt absolutely right.

When we both left *Wired* in the late nineties, we stayed in touch through occasional e-mails. Around 2001, we got onto the topic of our kids and their education. His kids were older than mine, so I asked him what kind of school he was sending them to.

"They don't go to school," he replied.

"Do you homeschool them?" I asked.

"No," he wrote. "We let them teach themselves."

I thought this was a little nutty, and I wrote it off as a quirk of an odd but brilliant person. But after having spent a little time teaching my own kids, I started wondering how Andrew had fared with his own, much more extreme home education project. I gave him and his wife, Renee, a call.

Today, the Ankers' three kids are teenagers. The three have never attended a school, public or private. When Zach, the oldest, was still a baby, Andrew said that he and Renee were concerned with the way that schools were becoming "increasingly ugly, regimented places." The Columbine massacre was in the news at the time, and schools were installing metal detectors and hiring security guards. More and more emphasis was being placed on standardization. Angry parents were demanding to know why their children's test scores were dropping, and administrators were reacting by increasing homework loads and focusing on highly structured teaching with an emphasis on passing standardized tests, instead of teaching them skills that would help them lead rewarding, responsible lives.

The Ankers wanted no part of that world and began looking for alternatives. It just so happened that the San Francisco Bay Area, where they live, is a hotspot for so-called unschoolers. Andrew says unschooling is popular in the area because it's full of high-tech entrepreneurs—driven, bright people who are creating online companies that develop and use cutting-edge technologies no school has taught because no school can keep up with the pace of the innovation. People like Andrew. When he was leading the team that started *HotWired* in 1993, there were no classes on how to build a commercial Web site. "We built it *because* we were untrained," he said. "I am at my most creative when I do something I have no experience with."

"Why don't you want to at least homeschool them?" I asked.

"Homeschools are usually for religious parents who want to insulate their kids from secular teaching," Andrew explained. "It's the same as school but at home. Unschoolers don't believe in schools. Most of what you learn in school is how to sit behind a desk and take homework."

"Is it legal?" I asked.

"Apparently, it's not really *illegal*," he said, "but states and counties aren't too happy about it." Andrew and his wife make an attempt to stay on the right side of the law by submitting an R4 form to the state of California each year, declaring their house to be a school. Renee is the headmaster, and Andrew is the assistant headmaster.

The Ankers are not alone. Unschooling is a movement based on the ideas developed by an educational reformer named John Holt, who died in 1985. In 1981 he told a reporter, "It's not that I feel that school is a good idea gone wrong, but a wrong idea from the word go. It's a nutty notion that we can have a place where nothing but learning happens, cut off from the rest of life."

Pat Farenga, who is carrying on Holt's work, defined unschooling as

*allowing children as much freedom to learn in the world as their parents can comfortably bear. The advantage of this method is that it doesn't require you, the parent, to become someone else, i.e., a professional teacher pouring knowledge into child-vessels on a planned basis. Instead you live and learn together, pursuing questions and interests as they arise and using conventional schooling on an "on demand" basis, if at all. This is the way we learn before going to school and the way we learn when we leave school and enter the world of work.*

The idea of unschooling isn't to make your home more like a school. In fact, unschooling proponents say that parents should try to make their home even *less* like a school than it already is. Andrew agrees.

It sounded interesting, at least in theory, but I doubted it would work in practice. I told Andrew that I thought my kids would sit in front of the TV or the computer all day if I didn't send them to school or teach them myself.

"Yes, that'll happen," he said. "It's totally fine to let them watch TV for six months. My son would spend six months at a time watching TV, until he got bored. And he did get bored, eventually."

Andrew admitted this was pretty scary while it was happening. "When we had a thirteen-year-old boy who didn't want to do anything but watch TV, we couldn't sleep at night. My wife and I would say to each other, 'Are we fucking this up?'"

Zach didn't show an interest in reading until he was ten and a half. But around that time, he was playing Super Mario 64 a lot and wanted to know what the characters were saying (their speech is written on the screen). When he asked his parents to read the words for him, they told him he had to figure it out on his own. Because Zach needed to know what they were saying in order to play the game, he taught himself to read.

"Very soon," Renee told me, "he could read at college level. In a couple of weeks he was doing everything. He is my child that loves to read the most and reads obsessively. My girls don't love to read nearly as much as he does."

Zach cracked the problem of decimals (the subject my daughter has been struggling with) when he started writing computer programs involving arithmetic with money. "Working with dollars and cents was what turned the light bulb on in his head," Andrew said.

I told Renee that another problem I saw with unschooling is that my kids would bug me all day, telling me how bored they were. "Did your kids ever tell you they were bored?" I asked her.

"Oh, definitely," she said. "They still do that! I loved it when they told me they were bored, because I would always say to them, 'Sounds like a personal problem to me. I'm not responsible for finding something for you to do.' I would tell them, 'You have everything you need at your fingertips, and it's up to you to solve that problem.' We didn't coddle them. It's up to them to take charge of their learning. I think that what happens in the early teen years is that they start building up resentment for the stuff they don't know and they go through this period where they kind of blame the parent. They'd say, 'You haven't taught me this,' but meanwhile, of course, they'd been entirely resistant to any of our efforts to help them. But gradually they get that *they* have to come up with the effort. With other kids, that might take them their entire schooling before college to get that."

Unschooling doesn't mean locking your kid up in the house. Renee says when her kids were younger, she would take them places three or four times a week: museums, botanical gardens, parks, ponds, factory tours. "We kept so busy," she said. "There's so much to explore." On Friday afternoons, the Ankers would get together with the seven other families in their informal unschooling support network. The other families proved to be invaluable for "trading off" kids when parents' stress levels hit the roof. "Sometimes I'd just call one of the people in our group and say, 'Can I drop my kids with you, because otherwise I'm going to kill them!' And they'd be like, 'Sure! Drop them off.'"

I explained how I had been tutoring Sarina in algebra and asked Renee how her kids learned it. She admitted that "you have to do some sort of workbook work to learn some things," and that when she sat her kids down to tutor them, she met with some resistance. Mainly, she and Andrew relied on their kids' own natural curiosity and drive to direct their learning. She said Zach was obsessed with making Lego models "for years and years to the exclusion of pretty much anything else," and her oldest daughter, Dagmar, loved workbooks. (My six-year-old, Jane, also loves workbooks and constantly asks us to buy them for her.)

Zach, now eighteen, is attending a community college and says he wants to be a lawyer. He developed an interest in legal affairs because he listened to a lot of radio news about the O. J. Simpson trial. His sisters, ages fourteen and sixteen, have also started taking community-college classes.

I asked Zach about his experience with being unschooled. He said that after Legos and video games, he started getting into computers. One of his parents' friends got him started working with the BASIC programming language. When he wanted to learn more, he referred to "books, what other people were doing, and trial and error." He moved on to other programming languages: PHP, then

Java. "Right now I'm working with LUA, a tiny language you can embed easily," he said.

"So why are you interested in studying law?" I asked him.

"Two reasons. Mostly you can argue, and the other would be it seems like a fun challenge to work around a set of rules—how do you get someone out of it or convict someone?"

He said attending community college took a "little bit of getting used to the first week or two, but it wasn't really that bad."

I still wasn't convinced that unschooling was a good idea. "You and your wife both went to great universities," I told Andrew. "Why wouldn't you want to send your kids to prep schools and Ivy League colleges, too? Aren't you limiting their options?"

Andrew said that when he and Renee had kids, they discussed the role formal education had played in their own lives and how it had affected who they were. "We are who we are not because of school but because of what we did with our lives," Andrew said. Neither of them felt that they were using what they learned in college in their current jobs. (Andrew is now an executive at SixApart, a company that makes software for bloggers, and Renee is a home-birth midwife.)

"My parents still think we're crazy for doing this, though," Andrew said. "My father's a doctor, and he thinks it's the most ridiculous thing I've ever done."

- - - - - - - - -

Unschooling was an intriguing idea. I didn't have the nerve to pull my own kids out of school and try it, though. In fact, when I mentioned it to Sarina, she thought I was nuts for even mentioning it. Carla wanted nothing to do with it. Still, I found the idea of kids' having more control over their own education compelling. I called Dr. Peter Gray, a research professor of psychology at Boston College who studies the way children learn from a developmental and evolutionary psychology perspective. I'd been reading "Freedom to Learn," his *Psychology Today* blog about education. In our discussion, he seemed to share many of Andrew and Renee's views about childhood learning.

"What's wrong with the way kids are taught in schools today?" I asked him.

"There's a lot of things that come to mind immediately," he said, "the most obvious being that our educational system is set up to train kids to be *scholars,* in the narrowest sense of the word, meaning someone who spends his time reading and writing." This is a poor way for kids to learn, Gray explained, because people survive by doing things. School, however, is about "always preparing for some future time when you will know enough to actually do something, instead of doing things now. And that's such a tedious approach for anybody to take to life—always preparing."

Another problem with the way children are taught today is that there is little room for individualized education. Gray sees this in the Boston vocational schools. Recently teenagers who attend these trade-based learning centers had to start taking the same kind of standardized academic tests as every other high school kid. Having to prepare for these tests, said Gray, took "away their time and opportunity to do the vocational things, the things that they're *good* at. They're being evaluated on something that they're *not* good at, and not interested in. The whole idea of No Child Left Behind is that everybody is the same. Everybody is supposed to be progressing in the same way along the same track."

The right way to approach learning, Gray said, is by encouraging play, "where you just go out and *do* things, and learning is secondary to doing. In school, you learn before you do. In play, you learn *as* you do and you're not afraid of mistakes—you make mistakes and that's how you learn. Whereas in school a mistake is something bad. In some ways you become afraid of taking initiative and trying things out for fear you'll make a mistake." What Gray was saying here jibed perfectly with what alpha DIYers tell me—that mistakes are the best teachers.

This fear of making mistakes is so ingrained in our culture that parents would rather let their children miss out on an experience than have them do something less-than-flawlessly. Years ago, Gray said, when he and his son were in the Indian Guides (a YMCA father-and-son organization), their local chapter held a pinewood derby contest, in which the boys built model race cars and competed to see whose car rolled the fastest down a ramp: "My son made his own, and it looked like he made his own. When we went to the event, there were these beautifully crafted, polished, brightly painted model cars. There was no way those little kids did any of that. But it's as if the whole culture is oriented toward this idea that things have to be perfect, and if the kid can't make them perfect, then you do it for the kid. That attitude is fostered by an educational system that really believes that there are right answers to things and the job is to learn the right answers before you try to do anything."

Children learn most of what they need to succeed in life by interacting with the world and with other kids, Gray said, not by sitting in a classroom trying to remember information so they perform well on standardized tests. Children who are free to follow their own interests will learn what it is they enjoy doing and will end up happier as adults, working in a field they feel passionate about.

As part of his ongoing research, Gray and his graduate students study the way children learn at the Sudbury Valley School in Framingham, Massachusetts. The school, founded in 1968, is unusual in that adults don't design the curriculum, grade students, or direct them to learn particular things. The children there are in charge of their own education, and decisions are made democratically, one vote per child. The emphasis at Sudbury Valley is on helping children learn without resorting to teaching them anything. "It is an environment that really calls upon kids to do what they want to do," Gray said. "What's fascinating is that in that setting they become educated!" They don't do it by "sitting down and thinking, like little educators, 'What is it that I need to do? What curriculum should I do? How do I educate myself for the future?' They're not even thinking about the future for the most part." Instead, Gray said, most of them are simply thinking about what they want to do that day.

Gray consulted anthropologists who studied hunter-gatherer societies (which existed in a relatively pure form until the early 1970s) and found that children in those societies behaved similarly. "Whether the cultures were in Africa or Asia or South America or Australia or New Zealand, there are certain commonalities among them. One of those commonalities is that there is no concept of education as something that adults *do* to children. The concept is that children learn on their own and that children need time to do this." Another commonality across these cultures is that children, and even teenagers, aren't expected to work. "One anthropologist told me that in the culture she was studying a girl might be fifteen or sixteen years old and married and she still wouldn't be expected to work, because she's still a girl. She needs time to play with the other kids, and there's just an understanding that play is how kids learn what they need to know and that they will become productive members of society when they're ready to."

But that doesn't mean the kids aren't learning or preparing for the future. "In hunter-gatherer cultures the kids are playing in ways that represent the skills, values, and beliefs of their culture. They're playing at the kinds of things they see around them. They're playing at hunting and gathering and making dugout canoes and building the kinds of tools that they use and following animal tracks." They're not consciously planning for the future, when they're adults and need to work; they're just doing it because it's fun. They're doing it because the adults around them are doing it. Natural selection favors species in which the young playfully imitate adult behavior.

Sudbury Valley has a wood shop, a photo lab, an art center, and many other different kinds of activities, which Gray said reflects our culture's "greater variety of kinds of things that people do than in a hunter-gatherer culture." Because reading, writing, and math are necessary parts of learning photography, art, theater, and woodworking, the children at Sudbury Valley become proficient in these areas, not for their own sake but because they need to learn them to get things done, just as Andrew and Renee's son, Zach, learned to read because he wanted to know what the characters in video games were talking about. These academic skills, said Gray, are "secondary to engaging in the kinds of adventures and games and projects that kids get drawn into."

In hunter-gatherer societies, kids of all ages play together. Sudbury Valley doesn't group kids by age, either. Most of the play there is social. "And when kids are playing in groups, they're learning from one another. If it's age-mixed groups, little kids are learning from older kids, and older kids sometimes learn from younger kids as well," Gray said. When the kids play sports outside, the older children protect the younger children from getting hurt. In the classrooms, kids follow one another's lead in what kind of literature to read.

I asked Gray what I should do when my kids tell me they're bored. Gray's answer was that I shouldn't do anything about it. He shares Sudbury Valley founder Dan Greenberg's view that the best thing you can do for bored kids is let them be bored. "Just don't try to amuse them," Gray said. "Eventually people get tired of being bored, and they find something to do. In our culture we have this view that it's the adults' responsibility to make sure that kids are never bored, that they've always got something interesting to do." Gray said alleviating boredom is the kid's responsibility.

As for my reluctance to allow my six-year-old daughter to indulge her fondness for playing on the computer for hours on end, Gray told me not to worry so much about it. "Playing on the computer is not necessarily a bad thing, especially in our culture, where computers are so important." In a way, Jane is simply imitating what I do to earn a living, just as hunter-gatherer kids do when they make miniature hunting bows. (When Jane was younger, she used to point to my computer and say, "I wanna do a piece of work.")

Gray told me that Jane's interest in the computer could be making her smarter, at least when it comes to abstract thinking. It's called the "Flynn Effect." The people who make IQ tests have to make the tests harder over time in order to keep the average score at 100. "The kinds of questions they have to make harder are the ones that have to do with abstract thinking. Abstract thinking is getting better and better all the time over the course of history." Gray said it doesn't correlate with schooling—the Flynn Effect occurs even if you control for the amount of schooling kids have: "Most of the people doing this research think it doesn't have anything to do with schooling. It has to do with the kinds of things that kids are learning in the natural course of life, even from TV and, these days, especially from computers. Because they're involved in abstractions all the time. Whereas kids in the past might have been playing with real, concrete things that you can put your hands on. And so they had more manual intelligence, you could say. Kids today are playing with symbols. They're manipulating symbols, and they're doing the kinds of things that require keeping everything in your head. As a consequence, when they're doing these tests that require your ability to keep a lot of things in your head and manipulate things in their heads, they're good at it. So you could argue that computer play is an adaptation in our culture that is helping kids acquire the kinds of skills that probably are more important to our culture today than they were in years past. That said, I also think it's a shame that kids aren't spending more time doing other things, too, that exercise their bodies, give them fresh air, get them out more socially with other kids."

So what can parents do to help their kids have a fulfilling, secure life? Gray said he favors a hands-off approach. The best thing a parent can do is to provide them with a safe place to play, along with "the opportunity to mess around with objects of all sorts, and to try to build things."

– – – – – – – – –

I felt that my kids were getting some opportunities to increase their manual intelligence by their exposure to chicken raising, vegetable gardening, and food preserving, but I wanted to take Gray's advice a step further and expose them to something entirely new, like electronics. My father was an electrical engineer, and when I was younger, I used to watch him work on electronics projects at home. He built his own stereo systems from the venerated hi-fi kit company Heathkit, and repaired broken appliances. One day after school, when I was eleven or twelve years old, I waved a strong magnet in front of the picture tube of our TV set to distort the image. It was like using Silly Putty to stretch the faces in the Sunday funnies. But when I'd finished, the picture tube wasn't working right. Everything was skewed, and portions of the screen were tinted purple.

When my father saw what had happened, he didn't get upset. He drove back to work (at the IBM plant near Boulder) and brought back a piece of equipment called a degausser, which allowed him to fix the tube and make the picture perfect again.

I was impressed by his skill and knowledge. He taught me how to solder, and for my third-grade science project we made an electric eye—a photoresistor connected to a battery and a small light bulb. Shining a flashlight on the photoresistor turned the light bulb on. Similarly, he helped me make an alarm that would sound a buzzer when someone walked through the door to my room.

My two daughters had little or no exposure to electronic circuits, and I thought it might be fun for me to teach myself more about electronics and let them hang around and ask questions or try things out. One morning, during the winter holiday school break, I pulled out an electronics kit I'd purchased a couple of years back but had never used, RadioShack's Electronics Learning Lab: A Complete Course in Electronics. It was designed and written by Forrest Mims. The main component of the kit was a black plastic box the size of a laptop computer containing a solderless breadboard surrounded by switches, dials, LEDs, a meter, a photoresistor, a buzzer, a speaker, and several knobs. The kit also came with a bunch of resistors, capacitors, transistors, and integrated circuits. The two workbooks, both by Mims, had instructions for building two hundred different projects.

I sat down at the kitchen table with the kit and started wiring up the first project in the first workbook—a simple LED flasher. The girls saw me and started asking questions right away. I told them what I was doing, and Jane volunteered to help me make the circuit. Sarina soon lost interest and wandered away to play Club Penguin, her favorite online social network at the time.

I showed Jane the bag of resistors and pointed out the different-colored bands printed on them. "Some of the resistors are like fat drinking straws that are easy to drink from," I said, "and others are like very thin straws, like coffee stirrers, that make it hard to drink juice. But instead of juice, electricity goes through them." She helped me find the three different resistors we needed for the project. I asked her if we should use a red or green LED. She said she wanted them both. "OK, but let's just start with one to make sure the circuit works, and then we'll try to add the other." She chose red.

I pulled a 555 timer integrated circuit from a strip of pink electrostatic foam and pushed it into the breadboard. I explained what I was doing as I went along. I pointed to the schematic in the workbook. "See, this drawing tells you where to connect the wires and the resistors and the light. Pin 1 on the chip needs to go to the negative side of the electricity. Pin 2 and pin 6 need to be connected to each other." Jane asked me how I knew which pin on the chip was which. I showed her the drawing of the 555 timer chip, and how the circle on the top of the chip was next to pin 1, and that you went around in a circle from pin 1 to pin 8. I was happy that she was asking questions. She had already learned a great deal about electronics in just a couple of minutes! "All of your toys that light up or make noise have this stuff inside them," I said.

I continued to wire the circuit, but it was taking a long time, and Jane's attention began to drift. I didn't ask her to concentrate, because I knew that she would rebel if I tried to force her to pay attention. She asked Carla if she could play chess with her—which Carla had starting teaching her the day before—and they set up the board on the other end of the kitchen table.

While they played, I finished the circuit, but it wasn't working. The LED was on, but it wasn't blinking. I checked the connections, polarities, and parts but couldn't find anything wrong, so I pulled everything apart and started over. This time it worked, and when I showed Jane, she smiled and said she wanted me to add the green LED. I did that, and we saw that the red LED became dimmer because the circuit was powering two lights instead of one. Another valuable lesson learned!

Sarina was plopped on the couch with a laptop. I walked over with the circuit and showed it to her. It elicited a halfhearted "cool," but it was no match for the action taking place on the disco floor in Club Penguin land. I wanted to ask her to quit playing and sit with me, but I remembered Dr. Gray's advice about not trying to force things on my kids. I felt like I was already pushing it by tutoring her with math.

# LEADING UP TO THE TEST

As the day of the test approached, Sarina and I continued to work together on the math problems in the sample ISEE test book. I concentrated on remaining calm when she became frustrated, and refraining from interrupting her when she was intent on solving a problem the wrong way, because I'd learned from experience that she would get agitated if I stopped her to demonstrate the correct approach. It was better to let her fail and realize it on her own, and then show her the correct way to solve the problem.

We'd been practicing together for weeks, and I was sensing progress. Now when we sat down to study, I didn't have to begin at square one as I had earlier. She had acquired a set of skills and knew how to use it. Carla was concerned that we weren't studying enough, but I felt Sarina was getting enough practice and didn't want to burn her out.

The night before the test we ran through some of the different kinds of math questions she'd be given. She did a good job. In the morning, on the way to the test, I asked her how she felt, and she said she was confident. When I picked her up a few hours later, she said it went well. Now all we had to do was wait for the test results. "I hope we did the right thing," said Carla. "If your experiment didn't work, Sarina's going to be the one who suffers."

"Don't worry," I said. "She knew the material. She'll do fine."

A couple of weeks later the envelope arrived while I was out of town. Carla called me. The news wasn't good. Sarina had scored in the thirtieth percentile for one math area and the fiftieth in the other, compared with the other students who'd taken the test.

What had gone wrong? I can only guess that Sarina had more trouble with the test process, format, and setting than she had had with the actual math involved, because I felt that our work together had really helped her learn fractions, decimals, and percentages. I realized I should have hired a tutor, one who would have taught her not only how to solve the kinds of questions on the test but also how to *take* the test: budgeting her time, when to guess, how to eliminate obvious wrong choices, when to move on to the next problem, and so on. I'd touched on a few of those kinds of tactics, but a tutor would have known exactly how to help her in test-taking skills.

Thinking about this made me angry. My anger was directed at myself. Faced with a choice of buying into a system I didn't like or rejecting it entirely, I took a middle road that ended up punishing my daughter. Carla and I aren't going to unschool or homeschool Sarina and Jane, so I need to accept the fact that my kids may sometimes need tutors who train kids to be better test takers.

My revised goal is to supplement their traditional education with as many undirected, unstructured, play-oriented learning opportunities as possible.

# CONCLUSION:

# THE RISE OF DO-IT-YOURSELFISM

"In almost all the varied walks of life, amateurs have more freedom to experiment and innovate. The fraction of the population who are amateurs is a good measure of the freedom of a society."
—FREEMAN DYSON, "IN PRAISE OF AMATEURS,"
*THE NEW YORK REVIEW OF BOOKS,* DEC. 5, 2002

When I embarked on my amateur adventure, my DIY friends warned me not to become discouraged by the mistakes I'd inevitably make. I accepted their advice, but I grossly underestimated just *how many* mistakes that would be. In fact, I never have stopped screwing up. Errors erupt like mushrooms in whatever project I work on, no matter how small or simple. For example, recently, I built some bookshelves for our family room. At the start, I felt as though I'd gained enough skill with woodworking that the project should be a breeze. After all, how difficult could it be to saw lumber, paint it white, and attach it to the wall? After a visit to Home Depot to purchase the necessary materials, I went to work with high expectations. The first piece of lumber I cut was two inches too short. And even though I used a T-square to mark the cut lines, the cuts didn't end up at ninety-degree angles. After painting the lumber, I realized that the paint was a shade too light—it didn't match the existing shelves. I poked around under the stairs and found an old can of paint that seemed to match, but it ended up being off, too. When it came time to attach the skewed, off-color shelves to the wall, I couldn't find my level. I downloaded a level application for my iPhone, which seemed to work pretty well, but somehow in the middle of installing the shelves I accidentally re-zeroed the level, so that it was about five degrees off-kilter. Then I discovered that I had bought the wrong kind of shelving hardware. I could go on and on about the errors I made over the next couple of days installing those shelves, but why embarrass myself further? In the end, though, the shelves ended up looking OK—under casual inspection.

At this point in my journey, I'm so used to making mistakes that I'm no longer discouraged by them. I know that, once in a while, a mistake will reveal a better way to do something. In addition, making mistakes means that I'm challenging myself.

When I started my experiment to become a DIYer, I had two goals in mind:

1. To improve my family's home life by taking an active role in the things that feed, clothe, educate, maintain, and entertain us.
2. To gain a deeper connection and sense of engagement with the things and systems that keep us alive and happy.

Now that I've been at it for a year and a half, I'm able to assess how well I met these goals.

Our home life has definitely improved. Gardening, tending to the chickens, and preserving food is a great way to spend time together. Jane especially enjoys working with me on everything I do. Instead of playing Nintendo Wii with her, we do a lot of gardening and food preparation together as we did before. She is always happy to help me plant seeds; make *kombucha,* yogurt, and sauerkraut; or tend to the chickens. Even when I'm working on solo projects, like woodcarving or cigar-box guitar building, Jane hangs around, asking questions and trying to copy what I'm doing. I usually give her pieces of scrap wood, sandpaper, and glue and she makes things at the same time I do.

Sarina, being older, is occasionally interested in what I'm doing, but she is usually more focused on social activities with her friends. At her age, who can blame her? Preteens are wired to be social. She does enjoy spending time with the chickens and has been helping me scope out a place to build a treehouse, a major DIY project on my to-do list. The time we spent together studying math was much more fulfilling than I had expected, and now I take joy in tutoring her on all subjects. She's excited about the memory tricks I've taught her, which helped her get a perfect score on a quiz that asked her to name the capitals of every country whose primary language is Spanish.

Carla was the least involved in the projects, but she was keenly interested in what was going on and asked a lot of questions. And she offered a lot of encouragement and guidance, which was invaluable.

Now that I am making and fixing some of my own things, I've developed a more meaningful connection to the human-made objects and systems I use. I'm practically addicted to working on DIY projects. When I spend an entire day online—blogging, editing stories, writing—it's sometimes hard to feel much sense of accomplishment. I'm just flailing around in a flurry of binary data—snatching bits, manipulating them, and tossing them back into the chaos. When I'm in this virtual world for too long, a feeling of vague uneasiness grows inside of me. But when I spend at least part of the day using my hands to make or fix something physical, that uneasiness subsides. I feel like I actually did something.

Making things and being the household handyman has given me a deeper understanding of the way things work. The small degree of autonomy I've attained as a DIYer has had a big payoff. I enjoy taking my time when I make something, contemplating the possibilities in each step of the process, and being fully engaged. When I'm away from my workbench, I often find myself visualizing a 3D model of something I'm making, rotating it in my imagination and modifying it as I would with Google SketchUp.

I like knowing that I can make something the way I want it to be. I'm proud of the things I make and use, despite their imperfections. When I haul my kids around in the wagon I rebuilt from scrap wood, the wagon tells me the story about the time we spent together building it—including my silly mistakes, like mounting the axles too close to the wagon, so the wheels rubbed against the wood (solved by adding spacer blocks). When the wagon acts up, I can pinpoint what's wrong with it and how to fix it, because the construction is imprinted in my mind. It took me all afternoon to make the wagon. In that time, I could have earned enough money writing to buy two or three brand-new, factory-built wagons. But I didn't make the wagon to save time or money. Slowing down was the point. DIY is similar to the Slow Food movement that started in Italy twenty years ago. The planning, selection of tools and materials, creation of the workspace, method of construction, documentation, and final product of a DIY project are things to be savored, not to be thought of as hassles or expenses. The end result of what a DIYer makes *is* important, but it's also a reminder of an experience that serves as its own reward.

Even if I'm unsuccessful in an attempt to get something done, like installing a water line to the automatic ice maker in our freezer, at least I gain an awareness and appreciation for it. As an amateur maker, I study how objects are constructed and the materials they're made of. The appreciation for the things we already have extends to a wariness about things we don't have. Now, instead of grabbing shiny items that catch my eye at Target or Costco, I ask myself if it really will make my life better or if I am buying it just because it's new. Recreational shopping, it turns out, is no match for recreational making. We're now keeping our stuff longer than we used to, trying to fix it ourselves when we break it; and when we do have to buy something, we buy a model that will last a long time or can be repaired instead of needing to be replaced. Because we take care of livestock and grow some of our own food, we're more observant of the environment and cycles of nature around us. Because we have achieved a small degree of self-reliance, we feel more free.

My DIY experiences have boosted my confidence about things I would have shunned a year ago. I've installed two toilets (with plenty of leaky mistakes). I've repaired and installed a number of electrical outlets and light fixtures around the house. I've started teaching myself how to program a microcontroller so that I can make a device that automatically turns over a jar of natural peanut butter every twenty-four hours to mix the oil and the solid ingredients. I'm not as afraid of new challenges because I know that with enough perseverance, I'll eventually get them done. It's a great feeling.

The most persistent obstacle in trying to achieve these goals has been finding enough time to do them. It would have been easier to accomplish everything I set out to do if we had dropped out of our current lifestyle completely, but we tried that in 2003 when we went to Rarotonga, and it didn't work out. So I have to squeeze my DIY projects in between my work hours and the time spent dealing with other non-DIY-related domestic chores, like house-cleaning, driving the kids to school, and paying bills. That meant that most of my leisure time was spent on DIY projects, which cut into my usual leisure activities, like watching TV, drawing and painting, and reading books. Fortunately, working on DIY projects has been so much fun that I don't feel bad about missing out on those other things.

I'm not alone in my discovery of the joy of using your hands to build a richer, more meaningful life. In the last few years, I've witnessed a growing interest in DIY projects. *Make* magazine's Maker Faire, a giant DIY expo held yearly in San Mateo, California, started in 2005 with twenty thousand attendees. By 2009 attendance had grown to seventy-five thousand. The pickle and sauerkraut workshops I've helped run in Los Angeles get bigger every time they're held. Our beekeeping club has gone from a dozen members to more than fifty in a few months. So-called "hacking spaces"—where people can gather to work with power tools, soldering irons, and signal analyzers—are popping up all over the country, offering guidance and workshops on everything from sewing dresses to programming microcontrollers. Corporations like Adobe regularly offer hands-on project workshops for their software developers as a way of breaking them out of their virtual-reality ruts.

The growing interest in DIY is charging a virtuous circle—individuals who make things enjoy documenting their projects online, which inspires others to try making them, too.

I've joined this virtuous circle myself. Whenever I build a new guitar or a new gadget for my chicken coop, I post a description or a video about it on my blog. Many people have e-mailed me to let me know that my projects have spurred them to do their own projects. They've told me that making things has changed the way they look at the world around them, opening new doors and presenting new opportunities to get deeply involved in processes that require knowledge, skill building, creativity, critical thinking, decision making, risk taking, social interaction, and resourcefulness. They understand that when you do something yourself, the thing that changes most profoundly is you.

# ACKNOWLEDGMENTS

This book wouldn't have been possible if not for the hundreds of truly inspiring people I've met through *Make* magazine and Maker Faire. I can't name them all here, but the following were especially helpful and deserve recognition: Mark Allen, Chris Anderson, Kirk Anderson, Gerry Arrington, Russell Bates, Gareth Branwyn, Daniel Carter, Laura Cochrane, Shawn Connally, Larry Cotton, Kelly Coyne, Collin Cunningham, Julian Darley, Roy Doty, George Dyson, the Evil Mad Scientists, Limor Fried, Kyle Glanville, Arwen O'Reilly Griffith, Saul Griffith, Bill Gurstelle, Keith Hammond, Sherry Huss, Tom Igoe, Brian Jepson, Kip Kay, Erik Knutzen, Todd Lappin, Andrew Lewis, Steve Lodefink, Kris Magri, Terrie Miller, Forrest Mims, Goli Mohammadi, Sam Murphy, Julia Posey, Tim O'Reilly, Mike Outmesguine, John Edgar Park, Tom Parker, Celine Rich, Phil Ross, Adam Savage, Amy Seidenwurm, Donald Simanek, Paul Spinrad, Becky Stern, Eric Thomason, Phillip Torrone, Gever Tulley, Cy Tymony, Marc de Vinck, David Williams, Katie Wilson, Dan Woods, and Lee D. Zlotoff. I'm especially thankful to my friends Mister Jalopy and Charles Platt, who generously shared their time and workshops with me, and who changed my idea for what this book was going to be about. I would like to thank Dale Dougherty, the founder of *Make*, for inviting me to join him and for providing me with many insights about the nature of DIY that found their way into my book.

My father, Lew, a DIYer his entire life, taught me many lessons that I didn't pay much attention to while growing up, but which became invaluable when I made the decision to become a DIYer.

Thanks go to my co-editors at Boing Boing—Cory Doctorow, Xeni Jardin, and David Pescovitz—as well as to the readers of the blog, who offered constructive feedback on my projects that I posted there.

The copy editor, Candy Gianetti, did a top-notch job of tightening my copy and catching quite a few factual and chronological errors, and for this I'm grateful.

I couldn't imagine embarking on a book without Byrd Leavell of Waxman Literary Agency at my side—thanks for being the best, Byrd.

Tim Sullivan, the editor who approached me with the idea of writing a DIY book in March of 2008, provided great advice during the early stages of the book.

I was delighted to have the opportunity to work with David Moldawer again, the editor of my previous book. David's guidance, creativity, and enthusiasm were essential ingredients in this project and I'm lucky to be able to work with him.

Finally, to my family, Carla, Sarina, and Jane: Thanks for putting up with me these past two years. I promise to get those bees out of the rafters as soon as possible.

# NOTES

## CHAPTER 1: THE COURAGE TO SCREW THINGS UP

24 "brain research suggests that making mistakes is one of the best ways to learn": Henry L. Roediger and Bridgid Finn, "Getting It Wrong: Surprising Tips on How to Learn," *Scientific American*, Oct. 29 2009, http://www.scientific american.com/article.cfm?id=getting-it-wrong.

24 "No one talks of failure as anything but shameful": Tom Jennings, "Fail Early! Fail Often!" *Make* 10 (2007).

26 "The astounding success of propaganda during the war": Cited in Alan Axelrod, *Profiles in Folly: History's Worst Decisions and Why They Went Wrong* (New York: Sterling, 2008).

27 "radio, a toy of the unwashed, became the musical instrument of the affluent": Museum of Public Relations, http://www.prmuseum.com/bernays/bernays_1939.html.

27 "women bought just 12 percent of the cigarettes in America": Edward Bernays, *Propaganda* (1928; Brooklyn: Ig Publishing, 2005), pp. 54, 71.

28 "Brill told Bernays that cigarettes were symbolic penises": Alan Axelrod, *Profiles in Folly: History's Worst Decisions and Why They Went Wrong* (New York: Sterling, 2008), pp. 95, 96.

28 "[strive] to bring about the satisfaction of the instinctual needs": Sigmund Freud, *New Introductory Lectures on Psychoanalysis* (London: The Hogarth Press and the Institute of Psycho-Analysis, 1933).

29 "Eddie Bernays saw the way to sell product was not to sell it to your intellect": Cited in Mick Brown, "America and China: The Eagle and the Dragon Part Three: Onward and Upward," Telegraph.co.uk, Sept. 7, 2008.

29 "People must be trained to desire": Siavash Rokni, "How One Man Convinced America to Stop Needing and Start Wanting," The Other Press, February 2008, http://www.theotherpress.ca/index.php?iid=9474.

# NOTES

## CHAPTER 2: KILLING MY LAWN

31  "The greatest fine art of the future will be the making of a comfortable living from a small piece of land": Quoted in Maurice G. Kains, *Five Acres and Independence: A Handbook for Small Farm Management* (New York: Greenberg, 1935).

31  "Mollison later said it could also mean 'permanent culture'": Cited in *Permaculture in Depth*, http://permaculturecanada.ca/joomla/index2.php?option =com_content&do_pdf=1&id=34.

## CHAPTER 3: GROWING FOOD

51  "a liter of petroleum 'contains the energy equivalent of about five weeks hard human manual labor'": Rob Hopkins, "Transition to a World without Oil," July 2009 speech, http://www.ted.com/talks/view/id/696.

52  "Hopkins explained that for every four barrels of oil we use": Hopkins, "Transition to a World Without Oil."

62  "Erected on stilts, with a single sloped tin roof": Christopher Kieran, "The Shack at Hinkle Farm," http://archrecord.construction.com/residential/quarterly/0801shack-1.asp, excerpted from *Architectural Record,* January 2008.

63  "seventeenth-century French chancellor Henri-François d'Aguesseau": David Fryxell, *How to Write Fast (While Writing Well)* (Cincinnati: Writer's Digest Books, 1992).

## CHAPTER 4: TICKLING MISS SILVIA

73  "Bezzera devised a steam-powered solution to speed things up": Barry D. Smith, Uma Gupta, and Bhupendra S. Gupta, *Caffeine and Activation Theory: Effects on Health and Behavior* (Boca Raton, Fla.: CRC, 2006), p. 19.

## CHAPTER 5: RAISING BABY DINOSAURS

94  "Twenty-four billion chickens are alive today": Christopher Perrins, ed. *Firefly Encyclopedia of Birds* (Buffalo, N.Y.: Firefly Books, Ltd., 2003).

94  "the most successful birds on the planet": Tim Flannery, *The Eternal Frontier: An Ecological History of North America and Its Peoples* (New York: Grove Press, 2001).

102  "Seth (he goes by his first name only), wrote an essay for the Canadian magazine *The Walrus*": Seth, "The Quiet Art of Cartooning," *The Walrus,* September 2008, http://www.walrusmagazine.com/articles/2008.09—the-quiet-art-of -cartooning-seth-comic-book-cartoons/.

105 "April 1, 1909, issue of a magazine called *Gleanings in Bee Culture*": http://books .google.com/books?id=4npaAAAAIAAJ&pg=RA11-PA217, p. 217.

107 "chickens still have a gene for growing saber-shaped, reptilian teeth": Ammu Kannampilly, "Scientists Find Chickens Retain Ancient Ability to Grow Teeth," ABCNews.com, Feb. 27, 2006, http://abcnews.go.com/Technology/ story?id=1666805.

134 "One Web site suggests keeping a 'very active young cockerel'": http://www .feathersite.com/Poultry/BRKBroody.html.


## CHAPTER 6: STRUMMING AND STIRRING

135 "What's important about this making stuff is": Quoted in John Kalish, "Digital DIY: Web Helps Do-It-Yourselfers Share Ethic," NPR online, March 9, 2008, http://www.npr.org/templates/story/story.php?storyId=87815753.

147 "the repetitive aspect of knitting elicits a 'relaxation response'": "Knitting," *Academic Medicine,* July 2001, http://journals.lww.com/academicmedicine/ Fulltext/2001/07000/Knitting.4.aspx#P10.

147 "Andrea Price, a knitting-book author": http://www.youtube.com/watch?v =Hpv07ZaGoHg.

151 "the master carvers of the misnamed 'Black Forest' school": http://www .blackforestantiques.com/black_forest_antique_carvings.asp.


## CHAPTER 7: FOMENTING FERMENTATION

156 "One book says it originated in Southeast Asia": Harald W.Tietze, *Kombucha: The Miracle Fungus* (New South Wales: Phree Books, 1995).

157 "In his 1968 book, *Cancer Ward,* Aleksandr Solzhenitsyn": Aleksandr I. Sol-zhenitsyn: *The Cancer Ward* (New York: Penguin USA, 1968), p. 165.

157 "An article published in 2009 in *Chinese Medicine*": Ola Ali Gharib, "Effects of Kombucha on Oxidative Stress Induced Nephrotoxicity in Rats," *Chinese Medicine,* Nov. 27, 2009.

157 "one study in Sweden in 2005": Py Tubelius, Vlaicu Stan, and Anders Zach-risson, "Increasing work-place healthiness with the probiotic *Lactobacillus reuteri*: A randomised, double-blind placebo-controlled study." *Environmental Health* 4:25, 2005.

157 "probiotic drinks could fight some kinds of cancers": "'Good' Bacteria May Help Stop Some Cancers, Say Scientists," *The Guardian,* Oct. 7, 2006, http://www .guardian.co.uk/science/2006/oct/07/cancer.medicineandhealth.

158    "a few sobering items about *kombucha*": Richard C. Dart, ed., *Medical Toxicology*
(Philadelphia: Lippincott Williams & Wilkins, 2004), p. 1750.

158    "In his book, which is part how-to guide": Sandor Ellix Katz, *Wild Fermentation: The Flavor, Nutrition, and Craft of Live-Culture Foods* (White River Junction, Vt.:
Chelsea Green, 2003), p. 28.

159    "ancient rituals that humans have been performing for many generations":
Ibid., p. 3.

159    "completely cut off from the process of growing food": Ibid., p. 27.

## CHAPTER 8: KEEPING BEES

163    "In September 2009 a *New York Times* blog ran an article": "Saving Bees:
What We Know Now," Room for Debate, *New York Times,* Sept. 2–3, 2009,
http://roomfordebate.blogs.nytimes.com/2009/09/02/saving-bees-what
-we-know-now.

164    "Every February, bees are transported to the Central Valley": Singeli Agnew,
"The Almond and the Bee," *San Francisco Chronicle,* Oct. 14, 2007, http://www
.sfgate.com/cgi-bin/article.cgi?f=/c/a/2007/10/14/CM2SS2SNO.DTL.

164    "There were 5 million managed bee colonies in 1940": USDA Agricultural
Research Service, "Questions and Answers: Colony Collapse Disorder,"
http://www.ars.usda.gov/News/docs.htm?docid=15572.

165    "Nectar, which is mainly sucrose and water": Kim Flottum, *The Backyard Beekeeper: An Absolute Beginner's Guide to Keeping Bees in Your Yard and Garden* (Beverly,
Mass.: Quarry Books, 2005; rev. expanded ed., 2010).

168    "Our apicultural forefathers": *Bee Culture,* July 2001, http://www.beesource
.com/pov/simon/10principles.htm.

169    "bee mites have 'all but decimated the casual beekeeper'": Glen R. Needham
and Diana Sammataro, "Bee Mite Biology," http://www.biosci.ohio-state
.edu/~acarolog/needham/beemite.htm.

169    "Thought to have originated in Russia": "Serious Bee Mite Found on
Honey Bees in Hawaii," *Science Daily,* http://www.sciencedaily.com/
releases/2007/04/070426113951.htm.

## CHAPTER 9: LEARNING HOW TO LEARN

185    "Every one of us knows, if we stop to think about it": *Psychology Today's*
Freedom to Learn blog, July 9, 2008.

186 "Afterward, Hahn graduated from high school": "'Radioactive Boy Scout' Sentenced to 90 Days for Stealing Smoke Detectors," FoxNews.com, Oct. 4, 2007, http://www.foxnews.com/story/0,2933,299362,00.html.

187 "You can't really blame the teachers and administrators": John Baichtal, Geek-Dad Review, *Wired,* June 6, 2008, http://www.wired.com/geekdad/2008/06/geekdad-review-3.

192 "a device to help blind people sense obstacles in their path": Caroline Williams, "Interview: The Outsiders," *New Scientist,* Jan. 21, 2006: 44–46, http://www.newscientist.com/article/mg18925351.600-interview-the-outsiders.html?full=true.

194 "this surprising discovery from a young, amateur scientist": Rebecca Lindsey, "Smoke's Surprising Secret," NASA Earth Observatory Web site, Jan. 5, 2004, http://earthobservatory.nasa.gov/Features/SmokeSecret/smoke_secret.php.

201 "It's not that I feel that school is a good idea gone wrong": Mel Allen, "The Education of John Holt," *Yankee,* December 1981.

202 "allowing children as much freedom to learn in the world": Pat Farenga, *Teach Your Own: The John Holt Book of Homeschooling* (New York: Perseus, 2003), pp. 238–239.

# INDEX

## W

*Wabi sabi,* 24

*Walrus, The,* 102–3

Whealy, Kent, 44

Whittling

consciousness, state of during, 146–47, 149

positive impact of, 152

tools for, 146, 148–50

wooden spoons, making, 144–51

*Wild Fermentation: The Flavor, Nutrition, and Craft of Live-Culture Foods* (Katz), 158–59, 168

Williams, David (One String Willie), 139–40

Wilson, Woodrow, 26

*Wired,* 200

Women, cigarette smoking and advertising, 27–28

Wood projects, wooden spoons, making, 144–51

Worms, in compost, 54, 68–69

Wright, Frank Lloyd, 93

## Y

Yogurt, making, 69–70, 160

"You pick" produce program, 53